NO TURNING BACK

Also by George Verwer

Hunger for Reality
Revolution of Love

NO *Turning* BACK

Pursuing the path of Christian discipleship

George Verwer

with Tony Collins

OM
publishing

First Hodder and Stoughton/OM Publishing edition 1983
Fifth impression 1991
This edition 1994
Reprinted 1996, 1998

British Library Cataloguing in Publication Data.

Verwer, George,
    No turning back.
    1. Christian life
    I. Title
    248.4   BV4501.2

ISBN 1-85078-250-4

OM Publishing is an imprint of Paternoster Publishing,
PO Box 300, Carlisle, Cumbria, CA3 0QS, U.K.

Printed in the U.K. by Cox & Wyman Ltd., Reading

DEDICATION

I would like to dedicate this book to the army of people in Operation Mobilisation, many of whom have stood with my wife Drena and I for over fifteen or twenty years, and especially to Jonathan and Margit McRostie. This past year Jonathan was seriously injured in a car crash and is now paralysed from the chest down. He is one of many whom I have watched live the kind of life spoken about in this book . . . yes, even now from his wheelchair. He recently spoke to 7,000 young people at Mission 83 in Switzerland and over 700 made deeper commitments to Christ and to the great task of telling the whole world about him.

CONTENTS

FOREWORD

About fifteen years ago I agreed to have some of my spoken messages put into print in the form of a book *Come! Live! Die!*, now entitled *Hunger for Reality*. To my amazement, since then I have received over 14,000 personal letters, most of which I have tried to answer. That book has now been translated into over twenty languages, so these letters have come from all over the world. It is especially with these people in mind that I have gone ahead with this new book.

As I reread, added to and subtracted from the material Tony Collins took and compiled from my message tapes, I almost decided to cancel the project. To my mind, there are already so many better books than this one. Being able to mention some of them in this book has helped me to press on with it. Mainly, however, it has been the perseverance and hard work of Tony that has made this book a reality.

I am constantly challenged by the way I see God use the printed page. Even in the past weeks I have found myself making a deeper commitment to the distribution of Christian literature. This firstly means prayer for people to develop a greater spiritual appetite. When this happens people may even take down from their shelves great books that have been sitting there for years, and begin to read them.

It is my prayer that people will not just read books, especially this one, but that they will learn to be a blessing to others by distributing books. Remember there are tens of millions who have never read a single Christian book, or even a portion of Scripture, for that matter. We can, and must, do something about this.

This book is basically for people who already know Christ as their Lord and Saviour. Unless you have at least begun in your Christian life through true faith in Christ you may find it a little difficult to understand. On the other hand, I thought this was also true of my last book, and to my amazement a good number have come to know Christ through reading that . . . so where you go from here is really up to you. And remember, what you do with the message of these pages will determine whether many other people will ever hear the message of Christ at all. God wants to use weak ordinary people to do great things for him. God wants to use *you*!

George Verwer

INTRODUCTION:
PLAYING AT SOLDIERS

The world is going crazy over short cuts.

America is particularly gadget-mad: the silliest example that has come my way recently has been the electric toothbrush. It is clearly too much to expect of any grown man that he should move his arm up and down; shortly, I imagine, a device will descend from the ceiling while you doze in bed with your mouth open, and hey presto! your gleaming dentures will be ready to face the world.

When, however, it comes to reaching the world for Christ, or producing a man of God, there are no short cuts. When the Apostle Paul said goodbye to the Ephesian elders on his way to Jerusalem, he commented, 'I consider my life worth nothing to me, if only I may finish the race and complete the task the Lord Jesus has given me – the task of testifying to the gospel of God's grace. . . So be on your guard! Remember that for three years I never stopped warning each of you night and day with tears' (Acts 20:24,31).

Whenever I read these verses I can almost feel the throb of Paul's leadership. Paul led the way in world evangelism, and those who follow in his steps will not be travelling an easy road. Jesus is looking for those who are ready to enrol full time in the service of the King of Kings. You can't become a soldier for a summer. In the United States army there is a system known as short-term enlistment, whereby you can serve for three or four years. The service of Christ is not like that. Jesus asks for a lifetime's commitment to the armies of the Lord: you serve until you die.

11

This attitude was plain in Paul's dedication. Now Christians use military terms very glibly, but we frequently know very little about the military life, preferring the easy and soft path of the holy huddle. I have been much attracted by the history of Britain during the First and Second World Wars, and in particular by the nature of Winston Churchill and some of the other leaders of that era. They seemed to have astonishing stamina, iron in their souls. Churchill promised sweat, toil and tears to those who went forward, yet they flocked to volunteer. I strongly recommend to anyone who has ambitions to be a disciple of Jesus Christ that they should read one of the books on the invasion of France – how the men came back from Dunkirk, recovered, and invaded on D-Day. They were floated across on immense barges and, seasick to a man, they landed on the French beaches to offer their lives for their countries and the principles they held dear.

When you read the history books it seems shocking, unreal, despite all the war films. Yet it really did happen. My wife's father was scooped up in a bucket and sent back to a nondescript grave in the USA. Maybe some of those who read this book will have lost fathers in that same conflict. It was horrific.

In the Mediterranean world of the first century AD soldiers and military installations were everywhere. Paul would undoubtedly have had a clear understanding of what it meant to be a soldier, and was himself no stranger to physical suffering. Yet he can write to Timothy. 'Endure hardship with us like a good soldier of Christ Jesus' (2 Tim. 2:3). Paul was not using words loosely. The choice that faces every professed Christian is this: are you truly concerned to be a trained soldier in the armies of the Lord, or are you secretly wishing you could be up in the grandstand, waving your handkerchief as the troops march by? To train and go forward as a soldier is the most demanding (and yet the most fulfilling) experience you will ever go through.

When I first set out as an evangelist, shortly after I was converted, my primary aim was to get people to make decisions for Christ. All my prayers were directed to this end. Nowadays I pray for and seek out soldiers: unless we get soldiers and mobilise our forces we shall never reach the world for Christ. The reason that most of the world's trained Christian workers serve amongst 10 per cent of the world's population (in the UK, USA, Canada and New Zealand) is that we lack soldiers and have forgotten our battle plans.

You are probably wedded to certain customs, to a particular language and food and style of dress. You may prefer a particular climate and culture. Most people do: this is why the missionary societies often will not accept older candidates, since they find them too set in their ways to adjust. (Changes are now taking place in this policy). It is very easy to exist in a Christian climate, singing hymns in church, praying and going to meetings and generally breathing the air of the Christian sub-culture. You may be considered a fine evangelical Christian, full of good theology and fine phrases.

And yet – there is little militancy, little conquering spirit, little thirst for risk, adventure and suffering. Do you think it is part of God's plan that the Jehovah's Witnesses outdistribute, outevangelise, outshine the Christians in just about every way? We don't like to admit it – nor to admit that the Mormon Church in Salt Lake City sends out more missionaries than all the Christian churches in the UK, Canada, Australia and New Zealand put together. They have 24,000 young men on the march today. Each of those men is responsible for the baptism of two new converts each year. Each convert, so they estimate, takes 500 hours of door to door visitation.

The Mormon Church is the fastest-growing cult in the British Isles. I remember a schoolgirl of sixteen I met in the West Country who spent four hours per day in evangelism. She came into one of the Operation Mobilisation meetings collecting names and addresses of possible contacts, and on her dress she had a badge with a big question mark. If you asked her what it meant, she would say, 'That is just so that you can ask me why I am wearing it, and then I can tell you that I am a member of the Church of Latter Day Saints and invite you to discuss this with me.' She was only sixteen, and yet she knew the Book of Mormon backwards and much of the Bible too. What is the average evangelical girl doing at sixteen or twenty-one? Ask the average evangelical boy.

Most people I meet have a stale Christianity. It simply fails to excite them. If you are young in the Christian faith, then be particularly careful to guard against creeping flabbiness. The middle-aged spiritual spread is a miserable sight. When I was converted in Madison Square Garden, many years ago, I got excited about Jesus Christ, and I've been excited ever since. Yet when you go to many a good evangelical church – of whatever denomination – on a Sunday morning, you sit there and feel at the end of an hour that you've just made a short trip to the North Pole and back. There is so little joy, as if we had been saved to sorrow: but in fact we have been saved to serve. Such service is perfect freedom, a freedom which is fresh and alive.

I believe that the reason many Christians are so dull and lifeless in their faith is because they are not in the battle, not using their weapons, not advancing against the enemy. Young Christians often seem like peacetime soldiers, sitting around, getting out of condition, playing cards, chatting idly. So many Christians act as though they were on a conveyor belt to heaven at the least possible cost. Yet God did not create us to live this life at a minimum cost. What was his purpose? Not just that we should be saved and thus get back to where we ought to have started: but rather that we should go on to conquest and worship and joy and life in abundance. 'I have come,' said Jesus, 'that they may have life, and have it to the full' (John 10:10). It is my prayer for the readers of this book that they should close it feeling that they can echo Paul's words: 'For me to live is Christ, to die is gain.'

The picture of the church is not all gloom. Here and there across the world I have come across groups of young people whose desire was that at any cost the sleeping giant should be roused, that an army should be raised up for the service

14

of Christ, that the commandments of Christ should be obeyed. This is what it all hinges on. In John 14:21 we read, 'Whoever has my commands and obeys them, he is the one who loves me. He who loves me will be loved by my Father, and I too will love him and show myself to him.' Yet most people I know think that if they go to church twice on Sunday they are getting rather spiritual: and if they go to a midweek prayer meeting as well they are getting superdedicated. Christians are commanded to pray: and yet prayer is regularly pushed to the closing minutes of the meeting. We have lots of messages and books and meetings and films, but few real prayer warriors. This deficiency hurts the missionary effort of the church, it hurts the cause of Christ; prayer is a part of soldiering.

We must not play at soldiers. My prayer for this book is that it should call you to effective service, and show you some of the disciple's weapons; that it should teach you how to press on when the going gets tough; and that it should help you to live a life of love – a life worthy of the Lord you serve.

PART I

The Call To Be a Disciple

1.

DISCIPLESHIP IN AN AGE OF TENSION AND FEAR

In talking to young Christians I sometimes end the conversation with a sense of confusion, a lack of focus. It happens especially when I have been listening to plans for evangelism, or when I have attended a prayer meeting which was long on enthusiasm and short on understanding. Christians are often from stable and comfortably-off homes; reasonably well educated; to some extent isolated from what they read in the papers. While they remain within the protected circle of their Christian friends, they are secure enough, but once they decide to deepen their commitment as believers they become vulnerable.

Modern society is not kind to those who seek to serve with practical love and in purity of body and mind. It is a fallacy to suppose that Christians are immune to emotional and mental breakdown: mental illness affects one person in ten in Britain at some point during their lives. But it is also quite wrong to think that if you do suffer a 'nervous breakdown' (which is a very inexact term) you are only fit for the rubbish heap. Perhaps God is trying to teach you something you can learn in no other way; perhaps he is giving you insights so that you can help others. The point is that Christians have to acknowledge real problems; you can't pretend that you are immune to immorality or alcoholism. If you are serious about your commitment as a Christian then you are in the firing line, and you will encounter the powers of darkness and their effect on a lonely and disordered world. Remember this when you meet other Christians who have fallen in some way: it is extremely easy to be unfair to those with emotional problems and to push your own under the carpet in a totally insincere attempt to appear whiter than white. It is very easy to lie.

One frustration, which is a cause of much despair, is simply the scale of the task of reaching people for Christ. Not only is Western society extremely complicated, but there are more people in Britain today than there were in the whole known world of the Apostle Paul. What do you do with seven million refugees? With one thousand million people in China? If we allow our imaginations to range over the numbers yet unreached by the gospel, we will hang our heads in defeat: and yet we cannot simply ignore the facts and concentrate on the local needs. The Lord is constantly pushing men and women forward into new channels of action.

The solution to these pressures lies in the *rest of faith*. The writer to the Hebrews comments, 'There remains, then, a Sabbath-rest for the people of God; for anyone who enters God's rest also rests from his own work, just as God did from his' (Hebrews 4:9,10). We are told to cease from our own works: to know that we are able to pass all our concerns over to the Lord, in the certainty that he can bear them far better than we can. In Luke's Gospel it is recorded that Jesus advised his disciples, 'Consider how the lilies grow. They do not labour or spin. Yet I tell you, not even Solomon in all his splendour was dressed like one of these. If that is how God clothes the grass of the field, which is here today, and tomorrow is thrown into the fire, how much more will he clothe you, O you of little faith!' (12:27,28). Yet a high proportion of emotional problems affecting Christians are a direct result of their refusal to cease from their own works, to stop worrying.

Peter tells us to 'cast all our care upon him'. This is a key principle to grasp right at the start of training to be a disciple. It is not something just for Sundays, but a daily practice which you must adopt to survive. If you cast your cares upon the Lord, and as you pray they come rushing back, then cast them up again. You may find it useful to keep a pen and paper beside you as you pray: as concerns for the day ahead crowd into your mind, write them down. You can offer them to the Lord and go on praying without fear of forgetting whatever it was that occurred to you. I lay such stress upon this point because I am a fearful worrier, and suffer daily from anxiety and fear and a sense of failure. My greatest help in Christ is that moment by moment I can pass my distress over to him. This is not a point you should agree with and skip over, but a discipline to appropriate for yourself. Without it you will find yourself avoiding prayer – and ultimately service – as too painful and burdensome.

In dealing with Operation Mobilisation business I frequently work very long hours. I could never do so if I didn't know the rest of faith. When I do not let Christ shoulder my worries I soon flag, but when I do release them I can work longer and harder with much less effort. Here is an answer to the frustration and despair which can floor us as Christians, since in doing so we become far more effective – and can lay down our burdens at the end of each day. Deal with worry as soon as you can, before it ruins your health and your life, and your home and your family.

We are not immune to the lifestyle around us. Have you ever stood at a station on a commuter line at about 6:30 p.m. and watched the drawn, strained, defensive faces stream past? The latest killer disease of the Western world is workaholism. There is no special virtue in working a twelve-hour day. We do not boast of being lazy: why should we boast of being overactive? Yet you hear people speak of their long hours as if they were badges of merit. One of the most advanced societies in the world is Japan, but along with their astonishing industrial record come records in other fields – nervous exhaustion, suicides, pollution. An article a few years ago described how wives would watch to see whose husband came home earliest from work, for it was regarded as virtuous to come home particularly late!

Christians are especially prone to workaholism. The Puritan tradition of work as valuable in its own right has been etched so deeply into our minds that we drive ourselves harder and harder. To work well is a good witness to our non-Christian colleagues, indeed, but we are very quickly in danger of working simply for the rewards of prosperity and promotion – and our lifestyle as Christians is soon identical with that of the people around us. But there is a further danger. The pace of Western civilisation has invaded our spiritual lives. The more busy we are, the more spiritual we must be: and so we fill our spare time with meetings. Bible studies, prayer meetings, committees can become a cancer upon the church. They are usually good in themselves, but they can so easily conceal from our Christian friends and from ourselves the emptiness of our faith. Sunday is designed as a day of rest, but for many church members it is the busiest day of the week. (If that is really the case, and you simply cannot avoid being busy on Sunday, then you should make sure that you take off at least half a day at another point in the week to relax and enjoy yourself.)

Frequently we hear the expression, 'I want to burn out for Christ.' In one way this is right: all we have is Christ's, and we are to serve with all our heart and soul and mind and strength. But there is a difference between petrol and coal, and I should prefer to be coal – to go on burning for a long time, slowly, steadily. Give me plodders, as William Carey put it. Michael Griffiths, Principal of London Bible College, considers that phlegmatics make better missionaries than cholerics.

Workaholism can stem from fear of failure, too. As Christians we can be sure that God loves us, each one of us individually, and we can find our sense of identity and value in this fact. Yet so often we feel that we have to prove ourselves, earn our salvation: and in this way too we show that we have swallowed wholesale the false values of our culture. Yet we all fail, and the more we attempt the more frequently we will fail. If we have been given a position of leadership we will fail very often. All the great men of history have made their blunders: Winston Churchill tried to whip the Turks and got fired when the plan came unstuck. At several points I was ready to abandon the

22

project for m.v. *Logos** as a total write-off, and though I had faith I was still ready for God to blow the whole thing up and make me look an utter nitwit. Failures are not all bad: you learn far more by them than by your successes. They are a springboard – as a source of theory they are far richer than victories. (Oscar Wilde said that the man who succeeds is the one who learns to survive failure.)

There is a further point to remember. Failures for the believer are always temporary. God loves you and me so much that he will allow almost any failure if the end result is that we become more like Jesus. Unless you see the hand of God in the ridiculous, the confusing, you may one day find yourself on the shelf. The Devil wants you reprobate, a cold, shrunken Christ-denying figure. Christ's message is one of grace for sinners, not of tonic for successful salesmen.

Please believe that I write this with compassion. I have failed far too often as a disciple of Jesus to be other than sympathetic: I have seen far too many enthusiastic young Christians get hurt when they tried to live in a truly committed way. Most of those who will read this book have to some extent led sheltered lives. In other parts of the world the pressure is far greater: how would you like to work in a refugee camp with dying children around you day and night? Yet even though our own problems seem so much smaller than those we hear on the radio, or see on television, God is still interested in ministering to us and helping us to find the way of peace and victory.

We can only ask ourselves to carry the light of Christ into the world because Jesus is constantly with us. He is at our side, ministering to us, offering us rest and comfort and love, totally forgiving us. building us up, calming us down, warming our hearts. If we want to live as his disciples amidst fear, tension, frustration, despair, loneliness, then we need again and again to acknowledge the presence of Christ. We need to tell him what we are facing moment by moment, to practice the presence of Jesus.

* m.v. *Logos* was the first of two ships (the other being m.v. *Doulos*) commissioned by Operation Mobilisation to provide Christian literature and educational facilities in ports all over the world.

2.

GETTING OUT OF THE FOG

We have considered some of the pressures that can hamper us when we resolve to live as disciples of Jesus. But there are more: the pressures that come from within. Many of the would-be disciples I meet seem to have drifted along for years, usually in the wrong direction, apparently powerless to make their lives count. In fact most of us need a turning point at some stage. Somehow we have missed real, revolutionary, dynamic Christianity. Pious words are cheap and easy to use, and get bandied around a great deal in Christian circles – and often disguise the fact that much of our zeal is borrowed and stops at the fine phrases. If we have been raised in a Christian environment in particular we are likely to know little of spiritual revolution. It has been well said that 'God has no grandchildren.' Our faith cannot be second-hand and survive. We suffer from the fog of spiritual unreality.

I believe real Christianity is genuinely a revolution, a revolution of love. This is what we have somehow missed: what the love of Christ can do when it begins to move through our lives and when we allow it to have complete control. It both gives a great deal and demands a great deal. We just do not appreciate this. Many of us are so deep in the fog of unreality that we can hear a thousand messages, read a thousand books, and yet never change.

Such a change does not take place overnight. It takes a lot more than prayers such as 'Lord Jesus, I give myself to you,' or 'It's just you and me, Jesus, and I can't do anything'. Prayers like this may be sincere enough, but they soon become commonplace. It is easy to pick up the lingo without picking up the light. Too often we want all that Jesus has to offer without letting go of anything of ourselves.

Yet there is plenty of negative teaching in the Bible. We may love to focus on verses which speak of pardon and wholeness, yet we should not skip over verses which read 'If any man would come after me, he must deny himself and take up his cross and follow me' (Matt. 16:24). Or 'Any of you who does not give up everything he has cannot be my disciple' (Luke 14:33). Most Christians want all of the privileges and none of the responsibilities. The Book of Hebrews speaks of the Lord as a 'consuming fire', and if we live the way the Bible teaches we are going to be ignited. This is not a comfortable process, but if we allow it to take place within us we will become a hot, sharp, burning revolutionary instrument in the hands of God..This is not the abnormal, but the normal Christian life.

You may feel by now that I am being unreal. Perhaps you have stumbled along the Christian path for years. You have heard all the revolutionary talk before and cynicism has set in. But what I am saying applies particularly to people like you. You are lost in the fog of unreality because your picture of the Lord is unreal. As J B Phillips put it, 'Your God is too small.'

To put it another way, many of us have a tendency to undervalue ourselves. This is really to insult God, because he made us, we are his, and hence we are of real worth. We are not willing to accept ourselves as we are. We may look in the mirror and wince, 'What happened when they gave out faces!' Yet if you are a quiet, shy, withdrawn person God is not going to turn you into the local loudmouth or the town extrovert. He is not going to turn you into me, and you can rejoice at that! God may indeed break and mould you, but your basic temperament will remain the same. A book by Tim LaHaye called *The Spirit-Controlled Temperament* is well worth reading on this point: it helps us to get past the pattern of thinking that 'I wish I were him'. (It is this kind of thinking that turns us into evangelical hero-worshippers. Because we undervalue ourselves, because our Christian lives aren't getting anywhere, because we don't think God can do anything with us, we turn to the big names. It is the Church's version of the worship of film and rock stars.)

If we desire to be disciples we must take this basic step of accepting ourselves. If we don't, then we are not dealing with ourselves as real people. Most of us know that we are not supermen, but quite a lot of us are convinced we are failures. Even the Apostle Paul had to come to terms with his own weaknesses. In 2 Corinthians 12:9,10 he writes of a 'thorn in my flesh' which the Lord refused to remove from him. 'But he said to me, "My grace is sufficient for you, for my power is made perfect in weakness." Therefore I will boast all the more gladly about my weaknesses, so that Christ's power may rest on me . . . for when I am weak, then I am strong.' Here Paul is saying that recognition of your own weakness is an essential condition of service.

Again and again I have discovered how true this is. Each day I find I have to look at my problems in front of me and say – with relief – 'Lord, I am passing this over to you'. But it took me a long time to learn this lesson and to admit my own weakness.

I am very, very skinny. One day – when I was still a teenager, before my conversion – I was reading a magazine, and saw an advert with a picture of a pretty girl on a beach with a skinny young lad beside her. The advert was for some expensive method of putting on weight and building muscles. The next illustration showed a big hulking character with bulging muscles coming along. He shoves the skinny bloke out of the way and walks off with the girl. This shook me up badly, as I was particularly interested in girls at that point, and I immediately wrote off for the kit. When everyone else was out of the house, there I would be, standing in the living room in my bathing trunks, straining to stretch the springs of the muscle-builder. After many months of effort I had gained scarcely a pound, was more frustrated than ever, and felt desperately inferior!

I used to put on a big act. I would go to all the dances, but all the time I would feel terribly inferior inside, especially in front of the girls. Then when I became a follower of Jesus Christ on 5 March 1955 in Madison Square Garden – Billy Graham was preaching – I discovered a whole new way of life. I found that God loved me. I found that he accepted me, all 124 pounds of me. I found that he could use me, not by crushing my temperament, or showing me up for the wretch I was, but rather by offering me love and working through me by his Holy Spirit.

This kind of revolutionary Christianity does work, and it will free us from many of our hangups. This is the real revolution, not running down the street with an armful of tracts or sailing off to Indonesia. It is not a question of working harder and more radically, but of being transformed by the accepting, healing love of God. The revolution begins in your own heart.

A Christian can be compared to a mirror. He has no light of his own, but seeks rather to reflect the light of the Lord. His ability to reflect light can be reduced by the fog of unreality, an unreal view of God, or an unreal view of himself. But there are other 'fogs', most obviously the fog of sin.

So many young people lead a double life. The Devil is no respecter of persons. Once a Bible College student came up to me after a meeting and confessed that every weekend he would sneak away and visit a prostitute. Most of us know secret pride in some area. Probably our sins are quite sophisticated: we used to gossip, but now we simply share prayer requests about other people rather freely. We bring a kind of evangelical aroma to our irritability and envy.

Envy is particularly prevalent in Christian circles. It is so easy to be jealous of another's talents. Someone else is asked to stand up and give their testimony, and you are asked to clean out the toilets. A Christian psychiatrist in India wrote to tell me that he believed that 80 per cent of people's problems stemmed from bitterness and envy in

27

their hearts. Perhaps we resent a friend or our marriage partner or our parents. Until we are willing – and it is a question of the will – to let the blood and love and forgiveness of Christ wash it clean out of our hearts we shall be crippled by it.

It is most unpopular to speak of sin today. We would much rather hear messages about inner healing. Yet it is featured on almost every page of the Bible! One of the main reasons we don't shake ourselves free of sin, but instead go on playing about with it, is that we simply do not hate it enough. Let me give a few examples.

We are snared by our materialism. We are extremely reluctant to pay attention to Jesus's teaching on this point. We will not face up to the fact that we have blinded ourselves to our affluence, to the cushy society we are living in. This love for material things is not easily eradicated: it takes a tremendous struggle. Tozer puts it this way:

> There is no doubt that the possessive clinging to things is one of the most harmful habits in life. Because it is so natural it is rarely recognised for the evil that it is. But its outworkings are tragic. This ancient curse will not go out painlessly. The tough old miser within us will not lie down and die obedient to our command. He must be torn out, torn out of our hearts like a plant from the soil, he must be extracted in blood and agony like a tooth from the jaw. He must be expelled from our souls in violence as Christ expelled the money changers from the temple.

The British and North Americans and Western Europeans represent the rich young rulers of the world (See Matt. 19:16). The poorest members of our societies are in the rich young ruler class by comparison with the rest of the world. Things we regard as dire necessities, such as clean water and medical facilities, are prized luxuries elsewhere. This is of course one major reason why European and North American missionaries have frequently been ineffective. Remember 1 John 3:16,17 'This is how we know what love is: Jesus Christ laid down his life for us. And we ought to lay down our lives for our brothers. If anyone has material possessions and sees his brother in need but has not pity on him, how can the love of God be in him?' This kind of statement is so revolutionary that it makes a Marxist look as if he's going backwards on a conveyor belt. I have heard Communists admit it. Yet most of the people who read this book will be drifting in the fog of materialistic society. I believe that God today is desperately trying to speak to the Church through books like John White's *The Golden Cow*, but so often we are not even willing to take the time to read such a book.

God looks at the heart. You may be very poor. Your poverty will not release you from materialism – if anything it will increase your desire for wealth. Yet if you accept it willingly it can become a treasured freedom. Most evangelicals have swallowed wholesale the competitive accumulation of possessions which is the value system of Western society, and this is simple hypocrisy. We may attend conferences and read books and discuss the deeper life, but until our words get put into practice and turn our lives upside down and change our attitudes towards one another, Communism will be more dynamic and the world will view it as such.

We are also snared by our impurity. You can fool your parents, you can fool your teachers, you can fool your very roommates; you can have pornography stashed away and be feeding your mind on filth. I would not make such comments if it were not for the dozens of people who come to me after meetings to confess such sins.

Billy Graham has called this generation a generation of sex gluttons. So many of us, for a few moments of pleasure, repeatedly throw away the prospect of a lifetime of spiritual growth and power. Yet if you really desire to stay pure then by the grace of God you can. Like most young men I lived for girls, for the next date – though, thank the Lord, I never did commit immorality, as I was saved at the age of seventeen, just in time. It would not have been very long before I fell to this temptation, as it was all there in my mind. Jesus taught very clearly that the sins of the mind are as unacceptable to God as the sins of the flesh.

We neglect or distort so much of God's teaching on the subject of sex. This is not the place to give details of God's plan for this most important area of our lives, but there are a number of good books available, such as John White's *Eros Defiled*. Whatever your depth of understanding, don't shove the issue under the carpet. Many evangelical young people have got hold of the idea that sex is dirty, something to be giggled over furtively or suppressed as best as may be. Many Christians have developed all kinds of hangups. There have been some tragic instances on the mission field, partially as a result of inadequate teaching. I know of several cases of homosexuality or lesbianism among missionaries: and in most instances a lot of the blame can be laid at the door of the whole Church for refusing to face issues squarely. If you repress your sexual urges, whatever they are, and refuse to talk about them, then you are making a rod for your own back. It *is* possible to be freed from sexual problems, whether lust or perversion, and yet so many of us are caught up in this particular fog. In consequence we shall never serve Christ effectively and may end up bringing disgrace to the work of God.

The right time to sort out this aspect of your lives is now, especially if you are still young. Roy Hession, author of *The Calvary Road*, told me once, 'If you think this is a big problem among young people, let me tell you that from the counselling I have done all over the world it is a far greater problem among those who are married with kids and in their mid-forties.' Simply getting married doesn't solve the problem of sexual temptation: it can make it worse. The Devil has no borders and the marriage border presents no more of a barrier to him than any other.

The answer is not to rush into marriage, but rather to open ourselves to the Christian revolution of love and self-discipline, of living in the light with one another, of being ready to face repentance. I know many who have been released from problems in the area of sex simply by opening their hearts and minds to someone else of the same sex, preferably someone a bit older than themselves, and praying with that person that the Lord will take them through. You will never get through by yourself.

I realise that this goes against the whole way we live our lives. We all prefer to hide behind the stiff upper lip (in the States it is sometimes called the John Wayne syndrome) and pretend that all is well. 'How are you today?' – 'Oh, fine!' But this attitude is very close to pride. In Galatians 6:2 Paul writes: 'Carry each other's burdens, and in this way you will fulfil the law of Christ.' I know that this is very sound advice. I would have left Operation Mobilisation years ago if it were not for the fact that practically everyone I have known who has been willing to share their burdens in this way has come through victorious. Learn to pray together. Seek to support one another and care for one another. This is a basic principle, and not just a once-off matter: nor does it only apply to sexual issues. We are part of the body of Christ and operate best in partnership with others. If you don't have someone with whom you pray regularly and share deeply – someone of the same sex – then see what you can do to find such a person. It is a great means to power in Christ.

God can indeed keep you out of the fog of impurity. If you do fall he will help you to get up again. This is one of the marvellous things about God's love: you know that by the love and grace offered to us in Christ you can be forgiven and made whole once more. It is most unlikely that you will get through the battle without a wound. When you see wounds – inconsistencies – in other people, do not be amazed or censorious, but rather watch to note which parts of your own Christian life bear scars.

It is not a quick process to reach even a small degree of spiritual maturity. It can take five or fifteen or twenty years of yielding yourself to righteousness, of reckoning yourself as dead. Pray to be hungry for Christian growth! You will discover that unless you first face up to those areas of your life where the Devil has control, you will have great difficulty in taking them to the cross and making your repentance have real meaning. We are very good at confessing in general, but it is extremely hard to be specific to ourselves or anyone else. Yet I do know from my own experience that the Lord can free us from the fog of impurity; and know, too, that without the freedom that he offers there is no hope of spiritual victory and growth.

Emotional problems are often a direct result of impurity. You simply cannot play with sin in any form without it affecting your mind. This especially applies to those who have been reared in evangelical homes or who have spent years in evangelical circles, as the damage is compounded by rebellion and guilt. You may have had such a rigid standard set for you by your parents or church that you utterly reject it as too legalistic. You may have had your ears so pounded with Bible verses that you have a deep aversion to even walking into a church. Perhaps you are sick of a religion that seems to consist largely of big cars, clean shirts and moralising. (Of course a man's faith has nothing to do with the length of his hair or the style of his dress. At one Billy Graham rally in Minneapolis, two long-haired men wandered down the aisle to take seats at the front, and were promptly ejected by the conservatively suited ushers. Billy Graham disagreed: 'I won't be preaching tonight until the two men in the audience who look most like Jesus Christ are invited back in.') Yet even if you have grown up in the smart-suit environment and turned right against it, you may still be completely healed of emotional problems.

For years my wife suffered severely in this area, with backaches, migraines, headaches and heart murmurs which were a direct result of emotional upset. Her own father was killed in the war and her step-father did not get on with her. Consequently she grew up deprived of love. When we met and fell in love she was still suffering from this early lack and was frequently prostrated by pain. Then one day she came across a book which helped her to understand that the compassion of Christ could reach into her and heal her, and this realisation led to healing where all the pills and therapies had failed. This is quite often the case. God will bring us to the point where we are willing to admit that he is sufficient. Our faith is not Jesus plus anything – plus a job or a husband or this or that spiritual practice – but Jesus alone. So my wife simply surrendered her life to the Lord and said, 'Jesus, I believe and I trust you.' She went to sleep and the next morning the aches were gone. She still occasionally suffers from past hurts, but now knows that she can be healed.

This is just one example of how the power of Christ reached into a person's life and restored them deep down. Do not reject this kind of healing as superficial. Doctors in England have suggested that as many as 50 per cent of the patients attending their surgeries complain of illnesses resulting directly from their mental condition. There are a number of books on the subject: I recommend *Healing for Damaged Emotions* by David A Seamands. Jesus redeems the whole person. Just as sin affects every part of our being, so the love and death of Christ are effective in clearing away deep wounds, resentment and jealousy, our failures to love ourselves as we should. With Christ beside us we can walk taller and hold our heads high, not because we are proud of what we have made of ourselves, but because we are proud to be made in his image. Whatever form our 'fog' takes, we can be free of it.

So often we are ready to speak of the great blessing we received five years ago. But what about the blessing we received this morning? As you open yourself daily to Jesus, he will daily fill you, making you ready for daily communion, repentance, combat. With grace and forgiveness nothing can stop us.

3.

FRUITFULNESS

We have looked at some of the factors which hold us back as we try to make our lives count as soldiers of Jesus. As we take our first wavering steps towards fuller commitment, we can be hampered by sin, or by an unreal view of ourselves, or of God; by deep-rooted emotional problems; by the pressures and false values of secular society. I will assume for the moment that you recognise the major difficulties you face, and that you still want to go on. You believe that God will help you find the necessary courage and humility. You are anxious that, as in the parable of the sower, you should produce thirty-, or sixty-, or a hundred-fold: that you should be fruitful. (In the context of this chapter by 'fruitfulness' I mean the making of new Christians.)

I want you to stop at this point and read the first six chapters of the Book of Acts. Please do so before you go on.

What was your reaction as you read? Probably you were stirred and you marvelled at what God did in Jerusalem in those early days. Did you feel that it would have been wonderful to live then and to see God so mightily at work?

Let me assure you that such things can happen today. If you live in Britain or parts of Europe or the United States you will find it easy to think that the Spirit of God is no longer very active in drawing men to himself. Yet in other parts of the world much more dramatic events than those recorded in the Book of Acts are taking place. In 1978, according to the Information Service of the Lausanne

Committee for World Evangelisation (June 1979), 6,052,800 new Christians were added to the Church in Africa alone.* The growth in Latin America and Asia is equally startling. Fruitful indeed!

It is clear that God does not operate the same way all the time in every land. Some places can only be categorised as 'hard'. It is very tempting to send missionaries to those areas where great revivals are taking place, and to ignore such parts as the Arab countries of the Mediterranean and the Persian Gulf. Yet God has not told us to miss out the hard bits, rather, to 'go into all the world'. This may mean the fruit will not come as quickly as some of us desire, but it will certainly come if you and I are willing and ready to lead the kind of lives and be the kind of people that God can use.

If you look at the ministry of the apostles, you will see that it is characterised by reckless faith. They were not daunted by flogging or threats or social ostracism. The truth in their hearts burned so joyfully bright that nothing else mattered.

Equally, I believe, God is seeking men and women of reckless faith today. He is in need of those who are ready to have faith that he will save the toughest cases; those who refuse to take no for an answer; those who refuse to be sidetracked into professionalism and bureaucracy and too much social emphasis. It is so easy to lose the vision for souls. No matter what form your ministry takes, if you have no passion for souls you are in danger of missing out on the essential urgency of the Christian message. If you have no time to drop your important job and tell someone about Christ, then you are too busy. It is a *sin* to be too busy. If you don't have the time, or the energy, to visit the local hospital and offer a little comfort, or to talk with the man next door, then you are too busy.

The first symptom of creeping busyness is often a cut-down in your prayer life. The prayer meeting becomes a discussion session, or a fellowship hour – and soon you are losing spiritual power and drive as you seek to do things in

* Quoted in *I Believe in Church Growth*, Eddie Gibbs.

your own strength. Prayer is the Christian's vital breath: without it you can't move.

The apostles were aware of the problem. They knew that it would be very easy for them to get sidetracked into the administration of the young Christian community, and realised that their first priority was the job they had been called to do: 'Prayer, and the ministry of the word' (see Acts 6:1–7). How many Christian leaders today are bogged down with paperwork when they should be out teaching, and guiding, and *leading*? The busy life is frequently barren. To be reckless in your faith does not mean to be unthinking, but the reverse – concentrated, singleminded in your concern that God should be glorified and souls won. Don't kid yourself and don't kid others by the amount you do.

I don't have as much boldness as I used to. Perhaps I am wiser now and do not embarrass people so much. Yet I frequently think that I'm in danger of getting too careful and tactful, and failing to rock the boat when that is exactly what is needed. I haven't given out tracts on an aeroplane, but Arthur Blessit has. He certainly annoys people, but who has won as many souls for Christ as that reckless warrior? His kind of boldness would have fitted well into the pages of Acts.

I am not advocating loudmouthed, discourteous evangelism. Apart from giving a bad impression, it does not work. Nor am I suggesting that you should be bold in witness without an adequate knowledge of the word of God. Nor am I suggesting that you confuse the energy of the flesh with the power of the Spirit. Yet there is a time for speaking out to cut across shallow politeness; and you must be sure that you are not using extra study as an excuse for avoiding your duty to bear witness; and you must indeed bend all your talents and capabilities to the task. If this sounds complex, remember that God can use even our blunders. The history of the Christian church is filled with instances where God has made use of acts of foolishness in the world's eyes to save men.

Without Holy Spirit boldness the world will remain unevangelised. We may hand everyone we meet a tract and a Bible with it, but until we get involved in the foolishness of personally preaching the word, we are not going to see very many saved. There can never be a substitute for the power of the Spirit working through willing men and women, and that power will bring boldness. Not noise, but guts to speak and discernment to know when to speak.

Compassion is an essential ingredient in this boldness. If you are giving out tracts or dropping hints about your faith just because you feel it is the right thing to do, then be careful, because your evangelism is a forced growth, a hothouse plant. Under such conditions we need to get down on our faces and ask the Lord to give us the compassion we need. If our evangelism is mechanical rather than natural then we are likely to be acting out of our own resources, and little fruit will result. Of ourselves we cannot make converts: only God in his sovereignty knows how to mix man's Spirit-led action with his grace. Paul puts it this way in 1 Corinthians 3:6, 'I planted the seed, Apollos watered it, but God made it grow.'

Allied to compassion, we need discipline. I shall be saying more about discipline in a later chapter, but for the present let me remind you that Jesus said, 'If you love me, keep my commandments'. Discipline is not a god, and Christianity is a religion of grace not law, but discipline is unquestionably a means to an end. Take letter writing, for instance. Perhaps you are in touch with someone who has shown a lot of interest in Christian matters. That letter which you never quite got around to writing might well have encouraged them to take the final step – but now you seem to have lost their address. Such little things count. Tracts have limited effectiveness, but do not neglect them. Always carry a few with you and keep some in your car so that you can give one to any hitch-hiker you pick up. Be careful to obtain those which you find the most attractive and persuasive; your local Christian bookshop should be able to supply you or give you addresses of organisations that will be able to help. My little book *Literature Evangelism* may also be helpful. These may seem minor matters to you, but just wonder; what if the person who led you to the Lord had also considered it a minor matter to strike up a conversation with you?

To illustrate the need for faithfulness even in tract distribution, let me tell you of a man I heard about recently who was going from door to door giving out tracts. At one house he had to wait some time before the door opened to his knock. The houseowner took the tract and slammed the door in his face. Later on, he called at the house again, and this time the man invited him in. He took him upstairs and showed him a box in the attic, and a rope above it: he had been just about to hang himself when the visitor had called previously. As a result of the tract, instead of hanging himself he knelt down by the box and gave his life to Jesus Christ.

Fruitfulness is not an optional extra for Christians. Suppose that a man in some Indian, or French, or Turkish village knew that you have the secret of eternal life. What kind of letter would he write to you? 'Dear Christian brother, I understand that you have many calls on your time. Your own needs are acute and I would not want you to put yourself out. But if at some point you could possibly drift this way and share the message of the gospel with me and my neighbours, we would be most grateful – but please do not lose any sleep or miss any meals on our account . . .' No! Rather he would send a telegram – 'COME AT ONCE STOP WE NEED YOUR HELP DESPERATELY STOP WE ARE ON THE ROAD TO HELL AND YOU ARE OUR ONLY HOPE STOP.'

Christ can make us fruitful if we are prepared to surrender ourselves to him. The more he has of us the more he can do. You have probably realised that it is quite possible to read such a book as this and yet never to surrender the larger part of our lives. As we die to ourselves, to our failures and jealousies and hatreds and lusts, we can turn our eyes away from our own sordid tangles to the glory and beauty and wholeness of Jesus. We will find that the lives we have abandoned to him are given back to us abundantly and with joy, both now and in the life to come. We are accepted not as soul-winners but as sinners. We are the grain of wheat that falls into the ground and dies, so that it may produce thirty-, sixty-, a hundred-fold.

PART II

Biblical Principles of Discipleship and Victory

4.

LOVE: THE HALLMARK OF A CHRISTIAN

We have thought over some of the challenges that Christ offers to his disciples, and some of the drawbacks that threaten to snare us as we seek to serve. This second section will I hope provide you with some guidance in crucial aspects of Christian conduct.

It is tragically true that a major cause of failure and bitterness in many missionary societies, including Operation Mobilisation, is the break-down of personal relations between members of the mission team. I am afraid that you are likely to know from your own experience that this is also true of churches at home. The minister or pastor is a favourite target for scorn and backbiting.

In view of our overwhelming needs in this area, it is perhaps surprising that we get very little teaching today on the theme of love. Yet many chapters in the New Testament are devoted entirely to this subject, and it is clear from even a quick survey of Jesus's instructions to his disciples that whatever we do or think must be built on a foundation of love, firstly for God and then for the brethren. Look at John 13:34,35: 'A new commandment I give you: Love one another. As I have loved you, so you must love one another. All men will know that you are my disciples if you love one another.' And in John 15:9 he says, 'As the Father has loved me, so have I loved you. Now remain in my love.' What an amazing truth this is! It is precisely because we are loved and know ourselves to be loved that we are able to love one another. As we love each other we show that we are disciples of Jesus: we are offering a picture in miniature of Jesus's love for us, so that the world may understand. (This is another aspect of the gossip and jealousy which eat at the Christian Church – we are giving a very poor reflection of the love Jesus bears for men.)

Love is the hallmark of the true disciple. If however we think that love will come easily into our lives we are making a serious mistake. There are two extreme views which are both common: that love is a product of extensive training and discipline, and that love is a natural result of a deep encounter with the Spirit. The second view is very widespread: yet as we grow in Christian maturity we must expect to go through 'dry patches'. These are valuable times, for they allow us to learn for ourselves that Christian truth is bigger than our own feelings. Speaking of this initial wave of love and enthusiasm, H A Hodges writes in *The Unseen Warfare*,

> This fervour is especially characteristic of beginners. Its drying up should be welcomed as a sign that we are getting beyond the first stage. To try to retain it or to long for its return in the midst of dryness is to refuse to grow up: it is to refuse the cost. By our steady adherence to God when the affections are dried up and nothing is left but the naked will clinging blindly to him, the soul is purged of self regard and cleaned in pure love.

I have thought long and hard over this. Of course new joys and insights which move the heart do come, and are welcome. But there is no point in bemoaning the initial zeal and love of twenty years ago – *today* we must deny ourselves and take up our cross and follow Christ, knowing that we are his, abiding in the Vine, for if we abide in the Vine, fruit will come, with or without a great amount of emotion. We have already looked at one major aspect of being fruitful in the last chapter, but there are others. You cannot separate love from showing that you love: and if you show that you are loving then you are in the Vine and you are going to bear fruit. These aspects are all bound up together.

Do not be led astray by the popular way of thinking that if you feel it to be right, then it is right. For years now hit records and romantic films and novels have been saying, in effect, that while the feeling lasts, everything is fine, but as soon as the feeling dies then it is time to move on. The Christian faith certainly offers plenty of joy and love and deep satisfaction, but it works from the other way round: do what is right, and your heart will follow.

There is another problem here that we need to be aware of. Some Christians find it very tempting to be so very certain about what is right that they start laying down the law. Often it is difficult to be both firm and loving. A W Tozer put it this way:

> It requires great care, and a true knowledge of ourselves, to distinguish a spiritual burden from a religious irritation. Often acts done in a spirit of religious irritation have consequences far beyond what we could have guessed. It is more important that we maintain a right spirit toward the others than that we bring them to our way of thinking, even if our way is right. Satan cares little whether we go astray after false doctrine or merely turn sour. Either way, he wins.

Do you know what Tozer means by 'sour' Christians? Often they have a good grasp of doctrine and a clear analysis of the situation, but seem to lack gentleness and peace. Any follower of religion can have a religious irritation: I remember an early meeting on board m.v. *Logos* when someone jumped up and began to yell objections to what was taking place. It seemed when I talked with him afterwards that someone had touched his 'holy cow'. It is very easy to be right in the wrong way. The Apostle James faced this issue directly: 'Who is wise and understanding among you? Let him show it by his good life, by deeds done in the humility that comes from wisdom. But if you harbour bitter envy and selfish ambition in your hearts, do not boast about it or deny the truth. Such "wisdom" does not come down from heaven but is earthly, unspiritual, of the Devil. For where you have envy and selfish ambition, there you find disorder and every evil practice. But the wisdom that comes from heaven is first of all pure; then peace-loving, considerate, submissive, full of mercy and good fruit, impartial and sincere' (James 3:13–17).

Just as it is easy to judge others, so it is easy to be cynical. We look around at our fellow Christians, and see all too clearly how far they are falling short of the standards they profess. Unless we are abiding in Christ – trusting in him, praying, worshipping, reading his word, opening ourselves to his love – we are likely to fall into the trap of cynicism. We read the Sermon on the Mount, we study Christ's teaching on love, and then we turn to our local church and see so clearly the lust disguised as censorship, the veiled ambition in leading members, the dominant manner to conceal envy and insecurity – oh yes, it's all there to find. It is very simple to see people's inconsistencies and to mock them, forgetting that communication is an art and not everyone is a perfect thinker with the gift of self-expression. God looks at the heart when people pray, no matter how clumsy their prayers may be. Cheap jibes are just that – cheap.

Please beware of a cynical spirit in any area. Don't be cynical for any reason. Don't be cynical even towards yourself. For every Christian who is troubled by pride, I suspect there is another whose opinion of himself is so low that it hinders him from seeing that God is bigger than his faults.

Tozer offers some good sense on the subject:

In this world of corruption there is real danger that the earnest Christian may overreact in his resistance to evil and become a victim of the religious occupational disease, cynicism. The constant need to go counter to popular trend may easily develop in him a sour habit of fault-finding and turn him into a critic of other men's

44

manners, without charity and without love. What makes this cynical spirit particularly dangerous is that the cynic is usually right. His analyses are accurate, his judgements are correct, yet for all that he is wrong, frightfully, pathetically wrong. As a cure for the sour, fault-finding attitude, I recommend the cultivation of the habit of thanksgiving. Thanksgiving has great curative powers, and a thankful heart cannot be cynical.

An essential part of love is generous service, the kind that is concerned not for your own status but for the welfare of another. Jesus gave a vivid illustration of this kind of love at the Last Supper – an occasion when every word and gesture would have been savoured and memorised by the apostles. After giving the bread and the cup he got up, took off his outer clothing and wrapped a towel round his waist. Then he poured water into a basin and began to wash his disciples' feet. This was the kind of task that would normally be performed by a household servant or slave. Luke records that at the Supper the disciples had begun bickering over which of them was the greatest, and Jesus told them, 'The greatest among you should be like the youngest, and the one who rules like the one who serves' (Luke 22:26). So, as a servant, he went round the disciples, but when he came to Simon Peter, Simon refused . . . until Jesus explained that unless he was prepared to accept he could not be one with him. Then Simon was glad to accept Christ's service.

I think that Simon Peter refused because of his pride. Jesus was challenging all his assumptions about honour and position by the task he was performing. Such things just weren't done, in Simon's eyes. He knew himself to have the kind of personality that others would follow, and he looked forward to receiving the status and respect of the world as Jesus's right-hand man. But his pride went deeper than that. It takes a certain amount of humility to allow others to do things for you: and perhaps in refusing to let his feet be washed he was betraying that he felt he didn't need Christ. This is one of the frequent stumbling blocks for those who are close to the kingdom: to admit a need of salvation seems like a recognition of failure – as of course it is. It is so easy to be stiffly formal and to conceal our needs from the world. Sometimes we will offer our help, but die before we will admit we need help.

What I particularly want to stress, however, is the kind of service that Christ teaches us. Most churches today have the bread and the cup, but unless we also have the towel our worship is likely to be a mockery of the presence of Jesus. If we go to the Lord's table remembering the Lord's death but not willing to serve one another, love one another and give ourselves to one another, then something has gone wrong. I am not talking about the sort of service that wins you recognition and respect, such as the Pharisees used to perform, but rather the sort that God alone knows about and honours.

The Holy Spirit will give us compassion and imagination as we open ourselves to him to see what needs to be done. But our obedience to the Spirit's promptings is a matter for the will. You may feel, 'Aha! I knew this was coming. This is where it gets hard.' In a way I agree: there are many different avenues for grace, and among them are training and self-discipline. But in this our human nature plays a part, for we are creatures of habit. You will know this to your cost if you have ever seriously tried to rid yourself of some practice which shamed you, like impure thinking. It is possible however, with the indwelling power of the Spirit, to cultivate attitudes of generosity and selflessness. The first few times it will be very hard: gradually it gets some-what easier. As you seek to love those who are to you unlovely, you will certainly fail at first, and be tempted to discouragement. Then you will start to see dignity where you had only seen foolishness, or integrity where you had only seen dishonesty. Equally, if you turn up early to put out the chairs for a meeting, it will at first be difficult not to hint that it was you who did so. After a while it becomes – most of the time – your regular practice 'to give without counting the cost' in some areas at least.

Love expressed in such generous service will really help

to bring about unity among believers. The jobs get done, the lonely and misfits are made to feel wanted, the minister or pastor and other leaders feel secure and valued. The whole church becomes more open-hearted and ready to praise and worship. Paul puts it this way, 'Let no debt remain outstanding, except the continuing debt to love one another, for he who loves his fellow-man has fulfilled the law' (Romans 13:8).

By contrast sourness and legalism will swiftly divide a fellowship. I believe that legalism is one of the greatest plagues of the church today. Don't do this, or that, especially on a Sunday – more young believers, I suspect, have been destroyed by legalism than anything else. Of course there have to be rules and principles in church life, but if we judge others to be unspiritual because they don't follow our particular set of rules, then we are making a great mistake. Love *fulfils* the law. Once you seek to keep all the laws of the Old Testament you are heading for extremes. Most of the false cults have taken their policies and regulations, out of context, from the Old Testament, failing to grasp that the keynote should be love. Once we start following all the laws of the Old Testament then we ought to adopt such practices as the Year of Jubilee, by which those of us who own land would have to return it to its former owners when the Year came round. By the same token, quite a number of us would have to be stoned to death! We should rather appreciate that the law of the Old Testament is to be summed up in the New Testament teaching on love. (Please note that I am not suggesting that the Old Testament can be neglected: it is the record of God's dealing with his people, Jesus quoted from it extensively, and you will not get a full understanding of the New Testament without seeing it as the fulfilment of the Old.)

The love we should show to one another should extend to tolerance of different religious practices and emphases. When Operation Mobilisation teams move into various church contexts they do their utmost to respect the customs of each church. We see it as really important not to be some kind of stumbling block to our Christian brothers. For example, I have been on teams in Scotland, which is a very conservative area and where there are many fine believers, where it has been regarded as highly wrong to sell books on the Lord's day. Naturally we accept this while we are there. Yet such a view would just not be acceptable in India, where people come to the churches on a Sunday from villages many miles around, and on Sunday many hundreds of Bibles are sold, for it is the only chance these villagers have to buy Bibles. Another thing I have noticed in other churches is the tremendous emphasis they place upon regular attendance at the Lord's Table every Sunday morning. I visited one church where you are given a little pin to wear in your lapel signifying that you haven't missed a Sunday's attendance in ten years. I really respect the dedication and consistency this shows: wouldn't it be great if we could put the same devotion into loving our neighbours as these brethren put into attendance at the Lord's Table?

For love is long term. When there are new Christians in the church we nurture them and give them our special care and love. But when someone has been part of the fellowship for twelve or fifteen years we seem to think that because they have been walking with the Lord for so long they will not be offended so quickly if we ignore them or make cutting remarks about them or make unreasonable requests of them. Their faith is surely so strong that they will be quick to praise God when they are not appreciated and their gifts go unnoticed. People do not grow less vulnerable as they grow older, however, and may indeed become more prone to despair or depression. Sometimes, too, you will need years and years of patient loving and acceptance before you can really build trust and a sense of worth in somebody who has been crushed by past rejection or failure.

Many of these thoughts are to be found in concentrated form in I Corinthians 13, the Mount Everest of this principle of love. Every Christian should memorise this chapter. Please keep it open beside you as you read the rest of this section. It deserves a great deal of study with the aid of a good thorough commentary, but for the moment look at the following:

> *Love is patient.* This can be deeply impressive to non-Christians, as well as being an essential part of the whole nature of love. It is easy to love for half an hour. The home is an area where the patience of love is essential: those of you who are mothers will know how much grace it takes to live with children and husbands. (My wife has a great deal of such grace – I am a very untidy person!)
> *Love is kind.* Simple kindness and gentleness are in very short supply these days. When we first set up the operation for m.v. *Logos* we found this was a real problem: we had to teach people how to treat one another with courtesy and consideration. Kindness is not just going around with a goofy smile on your face; rather it is the exercise of the imagination God gave you to see how others are feeling and to work out what they are likely to need.

People often come up to me after a meeting and ask how they can get further into the spiritual life. One method is by memorising Scripture – get steeped in the word of God. Another is by having good, close fellowship and talking matters over. Such fellowship means among other things giving freely, being quick to apologise, forgetting righteous indignation. If difficulties arise between you and another Christian then keep your mind on the primacy of love and unity: if a major matter of morality or spiritual principle is involved, then love and unity are all the more necessary. This is one area of life where we do need brainwashing – love, love, love all the way. Love is my aim. I know that I need many other gifts in my Christian life, but my primary goal is love.

5.

FOUNDATIONS FOR SPIRITUAL GROWTH

At the close of his second letter the Apostle Peter encouraged his readers to 'grow in the grace and knowledge of our Lord and Saviour Jesus Christ'.

If love is the dominant characteristic of the Christian's relationship to his fellow men, then growing in grace – growth towards spiritual maturity – is the chief element of his inner spiritual life. The two are linked: as you get to know God better so you find yourself able to love more generously; and as you seek to love more freely you find yourself searching harder for God and his strength.

To grow as Christians, we have to recommit ourselves to Jesus each and every day. True commitment is continuous, a fresh dedication of ourselves in the different situations and pressures we encounter, even hour by hour. At present I am the father of two teenagers and one twenty-two-year-old son. That is very different from being the father of three young children, or of three babies, and different again from the experience of being married but without a family. In each of these contexts I have had to discover afresh just what it means to be a committed disciple of Jesus. The kind of commitment that I had at college would not have carried me through the years that followed.

We could talk of a *habit* of recommitment. The way I trust myself to Jesus and offer myself to his service is based on all the other acts of·trusting that I have made over the years. It is helpful to try to see your life in the long term, to build up habits of this kind. One of my greatest burdens for young Christians in particular is to encourage them in continuity and consistency of life. I am not interested in seeing people following Christ just for one year.

Yet unless you get a firm footing to your Christianity, a good strong foundation, that is exactly what is likely to happen. Even if you do doggedly continue, without a strong footing you will be just a house built on sand. Short-term Christians are terribly common in the fast pace of the industrialised world. In Singapore, for example, where there are large numbers of young people in the churches, the drop-out rate can be as high as 75 per cent. Once they get married, develop a career and start a family, they don't darken the doors of the church any more. (The problem is not confined to Singapore.) Christians are needed who will stick at it year after year, realising that the Devil changes his tactics, and that each day presents a new challenge.

Let us go over some of the basic foundation stones.

First of all, be sure that *you are God's child.* 'I write these things to you who believe in the name of the Son of God so that you may know that you have eternal life' (I John 5:13). If you are going to grow, you need to be completely sure that you are born again, that your sins are forgiven. Perhaps this seems obvious, but in much of the counselling that I have been involved with, I have found that many people are not really sure of their own salvation. They've had failure in their lives, they've not seen the fruit they hoped for, either in terms of evangelising others or in their own characters, they've wrestled with their own ugly emotions, they've heard arguments against the Christian faith without thinking them through, and all these things have led them to doubt their salvation.

We badly need to re-emphasise the doctrine of justification by faith. This is the answer: no amount of failure or stormy emotion can take us away from Jesus – he knows all too well that we are failures! But some pride within us is always reluctant to accept that grace is utterly free, and again and again you find churches which have lost sight of this truth. For so many people it is justification by faith plus works, or rules, or church attendance, or baptism. This is a major error which denies the whole basis of our faith. It is the subject of the whole of Paul's letter to the Galatians.

I think it is quite normal for all of us to wonder from time to time whether we are really saved. Billy Graham said once that some years ago he went off by himself into the mountains for a few days to make sure of this very point: that he really knew Jesus Christ as his personal Lord and Saviour. If Billy Graham, who has led so many tens of thousands of people to the Lord, feels at times the need to search his heart, then perhaps we should not be too worried if we also sometimes feel the need to search our own.

When this happens we should always go straight back to the word of God, and to its clear, simple teaching that salvation is by faith alone. Now this faith is bound to be tested, and doubts will come. In one way these are to be welcomed, for deep faith is not produced in the absence of doubt, but rather as we battle through our doubts. Not only will you probably doubt (if you haven't already) your own salvation, but you are also likely to doubt whether any of this Christianity business is true – God, the Bible, salvation, everything. If you have a brain and are using it, then doubts will come, especially if you have something to do with psychology, or philosophy, or history as it is often taught. This is precisely why I think it is good for Christians to be involved in all these areas, so that there are no no-go areas of intellectual activity.

In this context I would like to recommend two books by Josh MacDowell entitled *Evidence that Demands a Verdict* and *More Evidence that Demands a Verdict*. These set out to present good intellectual grounds for faith in Christ. Josh MacDowell has led not only many, many students but also quite a few professors and liberal pastors to the Lord. The second volume deals with some issues raised by 'higher criticism' that has damaged the faith of theology students. Intellectual doubts can be answered – though we should be aware that a lot of our so-called intellectual doubts are simply big emotional struggles in disguise.

Often simple obedience is at the root of the matter. Once we begin to really obey God and hence to see fruit in our lives, then we gain a greater assurance. In one way God does not allow us to have all the assurance we would like if we are living a defeated, disobedient life. If there are areas where we are clearly conscious of disobedience then we just don't deserve to have complete assurance, and it would not be a kindness on the Lord's part to give it to us. We deserve rather to be somewhat on edge about things and that will drive us back to him, and to the cross. Use your doubts, then. Don't take to your heels.

Secondly, be sure that *the Bible is God's Word*. 'All Scripture is God-breathed and is useful for teaching, rebuking, correcting and training in righteousness, so that the man of God may be thoroughly equipped for every good work' (2 Timothy 3:16,17). The two books by Josh Mac-Dowell give a lot of good grounds as to why we can know that the Bible is true. There are certainly plenty of problems for the man who decides to accept Jesus's own view of the Old Testament – that it was fully inspired – and we would be foolish and unrealistic to pretend otherwise. It is a matter of great controversy. Yet there is a good deal of archaeological evidence that has come to light in the past thirty years that enables us to say with confidence that the Old Testament relates real history. I remember hearing Dr Francis Schaeffer speak about the problems that arise for the man who *doesn't* believe in the Bible, and I think these are far greater, intellectually and in every other way.

There have been low points in my life when I have been tempted to throw the whole Christian business in and go back to the world, but each time I have realised I just couldn't do it. It would be like running into a brick wall. I knew the truth of God, and the intellectual facts concerning the faith, and though there were some problems, in particular some passages in the Old Testament that I found hard to swallow, the problems were far greater if I tried to say that this is not God's world or that a personal God does not exist.

I frequently ask at meetings how many people have read the Bible through from Genesis to Revelations. As a rule the answer is less than 10 per cent. Yet you find people saying quite confidently that the Bible is not truly inspired, and when you question them they admit that they have not read it in anything like such detail. Before you reach a verdict you should examine the evidence. If you have not yet done so, may I encourage you to read the Bible right through, so as to get an overall view of God's purposes and acts in history? It is a remarkable boost to your faith: you will wonder when you have done so why ever you did not do it before.

The truth of the Bible was my great area of struggle during my first year at college. I was at a college where some of the teachers were agnostics, and they took a particular delight in tearing apart anyone who believed in the Bible. I was a very young Christian, and I had to wrestle hard to find out what I believed. In the process I realised that the truths that it contained, if they were true, were so great – heaven, hell, Jesus, the Second Coming – that I would have to commit myself to them heart, mind and soul. When, in due course, I reached the conclusion that the Bible was indeed to be trusted, I had no choice but to go ahead and make that commitment.

Without this conviction about the Bible there would be no Operation Mobilisation. It is a conviction that leads us and many a missionary to do things that we would not otherwise choose to do. Some seem to think that there is such a person as the 'missionary type', who wants to live in climates he doesn't like, eating food he can't stand! They seem to believe that we are evangelical masochists. Yet on the basis of the Bible missionaries have given themselves to the Lord, and he is the one who tells them where they must go and what they must be.

Confidence in the Bible makes radicals of us all. It is this that the churches of Britain and the USA in particular need: there are so many people who give lip service to the authority of Scripture, but do not allow it to dig into their lives. (I have never heard so many people justifying the status quo!) It has been a characteristic of great men of faith in every age that they had a high view of Scripture. Samuel Logan Brengle, an early leader of The Salvation Army and a notable evangelist, wrote of the fire that the Spirit who inspired the Bible lights within us:

> What is fire? It is love, it is faith, it is hope, it is passion, purpose, determination, it is utter devotion, it is divine discontent with formality, ceremonialism, lukewarmness, indifference, sham, noise, parade and spiritual death. It is singleness of eye, and a consecration unto death. It is God the Holy Ghost burning in and through a humble, holy, faithful man.

I feel broken in pieces when I read of the lives of some of the great heroes of faith such as Brengle, and see not only what they said but how they lived. It can all be traced back to the fact that these men believed that the Bible was God's word.

Billy Graham has told how he once had a deep crisis of faith over the trustworthiness of the Old Testament, and went away by himself to think it through. This was in the days before he became well known, and the decision he would reach was to be crucial for the whole of his future work. In the end as he worked through the arguments he came to a position of trust in the Bible, and went back to the preparations for his Los Angeles Crusade which was the beginning of his amazing ministry.

In the end the decision to trust is one of faith, not mental assent. This is important; without faith and love your Christianity will be a hollow thing, no matter what its intellectual credibility.

Without a firm foundation on the Bible we shall find it impossible to develop sound doctrine. Leading a man to Christ is only the start of the process: we must ensure that that man is grounded in Scripture, loved and encouraged in the faith. It is essential to care for and cherish those who come to faith so that they may grow: a major part of spiritual growth is precisely a good grasp of doctrine. Without it you will be swayed and confused by each new idea and each one-sided sect. But more than this, sound doctrine is a splendid avenue to a deeper knowledge of God himself, for doctrine concerns the nature and purpose of God, and can be a subject which is a joy to study.

The third foundation stone is *a correct view of God himself*. In Isaiah 6 the prophet records how he was called and commissioned by God. Before the Lord could send him out to make a start upon his long and harsh ministry, he needed to give him a deep experience of himself. 'In the year that King Uzziah died, I saw the Lord seated on a throne, high and exalted, and the train of his robe filled the temple. . . "Woe to me!" I cried. "I am ruined! For I am a man of unclean lips, and I live among a people of unclean lips, and my eyes have seen the King, the Lord Almighty"' (6:1,5). This was exactly the right response for Isaiah to make as he faced the holiness of God, and also the right response for us. But Isaiah also met the mercy of God as the coal from the altar touched his mouth, and in consequence was able to say, 'Here am I. Send me!'

We too need to encounter both God's holiness and God's mercy. Many people, young and old alike, seem to have a concept of God as a stern father figure up there with a big stick, ready to hit them as soon as they do anything wrong. Sometimes this can be traced back to a bad relationship with their own fathers, or to the fact that they have had little contact with their fathers in this world of soaring divorce rates. Under such conditions it takes time and profound healing to get free of false ideas about God. It is very easy to stress the 'thou shalt nots' of this Christian faith and to forget that the Lord who made you and saved you also loves you. If you reduce your spiritual understanding to rules and regulations, then you have become a legalist. Legalism is one of the chief enemies of the spiritual life, a key weapon which Satan the accuser uses to load us down with guilt. It will probably stay this way until Jesus comes..

The legalism that results from a false view of God creates

pressures on people to pretend. Thus they constantly try to give the impression that they are up, up, up, when really they are down, down, down. Therefore they grow unwilling to share their problems, even with themselves, and the drain that results upon their personality and emotions puts paid to any hope of spiritual growth and health.

A sound view of God develops as a result of steady reading in his word, with attendant thought and prayer. There are many good books to help you to organise and develop your understanding, and I would particularly recommend J I Packer's *Knowing God*. But the subject demands a lifetime's study: fortunately the Holy Spirit is a good teacher.

Our fourth foundation is a *correct view of ourselves*. This is exceedingly important, but as I have dealt with the matter at some length in chapters one and two, I will only touch on it briefly now. Some people think more highly of themselves than they really should, and pride in all its forms can be dangerous in the spiritual life. But there are others, I think the majority of us, who are suffering rather from a very low image of themselves.

As a result they are afraid to witness and to launch out into doing new things for God. Jesus told us to love our neighbours as ourselves – but how can you do this without loving yourself? If you do not like or respect yourself, then you will be hampered in trying to like and respect others. A lot of people are unable to relate to those around them because they are unable to relate to themselves. Years ago the Devil's primary tactic seemed to be to kill Christians in the arenas, through persecution, on the mission field. Today he seems concerned to maim and disable. The amount of depression, self-rejection and mental illness there is today among both Christians and non-Christians is unbelievable.

Now, I get scared when anyone starts coming up with simple easy answers when the world's best medical and pastoral brains have not solved the problem. However I do know that prevention is better than cure. Every Christian can learn how to rest in the Lord and to cast every burden upon him, to deal as seriously and as radically with worry as you would deal with fornication. I regard worry in some ways as a greater evil today than lust. Whether it is worry over legitimate matters or worry over shadows, it can still break you mentally. Our academic systems are so rough on people, and can instil such a sense of failure, that some of the best brains we have are rusting on the shelves of mental hospitals.

If you are obsessed with worry and failure then you are leaving God out of the picture, and that is very much a wrong view of yourself. If God has given you a good mind, use it, but don't sacrifice your emotional and spiritual life in the process. It is not worth it. Better the most menial occupation you can imagine, if it preserves in you a healthy mind. 'For God did not give us a spirit of timidity, but a spirit of power, of love and of self-discipline' (2 Timothy 1:7).

The fifth foundation is a very practical one: simply *allowing time* – time for studying God's word, for prayer, for witness and fellowship. All four are essential if you are going to maintain a spiritual life. Like taking a leg off a chair, your spiritual life will keel over if you neglect any one area. If you look at the picture of the early church in Acts you can see these principles very clearly. 'They devoted themselves to the apostles' teaching and to the fellowship, to the breaking of bread and to prayer' (Acts 2:42). And soon they were moving out into the whole region, witnessing. These are basic means of grace.

I would like to stress again the value of memorising Scripture. The psalmist said, 'I have hid thy word in my heart, O Lord, that I might not sin against you.' When I was first converted I had enormous problems, especially in the areas of lust and impatience, and felt at times that I was bound to blow my whole faith sky high. The thing that helped me the most on a practical level was intense memorisation of the word of God. The Navigators have emphasised this, as have many other Christian groups, but if you ask the average Christian today what he does for his quiet time he will tell you that he reads a page from *Daily Light*, perhaps reads a bit of a psalm and goes off to work. That is not Jesus's way: when tempted in the wilderness he rebuked the Devil using the words of Scripture, and his teaching shows clearly how thoroughly he knew the Old Testament. A well-stocked memory is a powerful weapon, both in defence against temptation and in witnessing.

If you are going to set aside time you will have to make a special effort. For some it will mean getting to bed a little earlier, so that you can rise at six or six-thirty to read and pray. It is so easy for us, especially the activist types, to put our relationship with people ahead of our relationship with God. If you are of a more mystical nature you may find it easier to hide in your cupboard with a torch and a Bible! The average person is a more social animal, and time for God means disciplined living, saying no to the body and yes to God. Alan Redpath has said that the greatest challenge to Christians is blanket victory – getting the blankets off in the morning.

Sixthly and lastly, *accepting God's pattern for your life*. Paul wrote to the Philippians, 'In all my prayers for all of you, I always pray with joy because of your partnership in the gospel from the first day until now, being confident of this, that he who began a good work in you will carry it on to completion until the day of Christ Jesus' (1:4–6).

That 'good work' goes forward at the Lord's own pace. Moreover, it is a matter between ourselves and God. We can never know how far another person has progressed spiritually, and it is futile to try and make such judgments. Never assume you know another person's spiritual status, for good or ill: I have seen far too many bright Christian stars who have suddenly fallen, with their lives in a mess and their marriages ending in the divorce courts.

Some people throw away their faith because they do not seek to discover God's pattern, and are too impatient to wait until it is revealed to them. They aim so high, and demand extraordinary things of themselves, and when they don't get there in one year they turn away in disgust, convinced that Christianity doesn't work. You will come across people who have tried all the techniques, and have had hands laid on them, and have tried all the different churches, and yet have rejected their faith after one or two years because they are still falling into sin in some particular area.

This comes from trying to push God into a corner, telling him how he ought to be working. But perhaps God isn't planning to release you from whatever sin you have right away: perhaps he is trying to teach you that failure is often the back door to success in the long run, that cleansing and forgiveness are a major part of Christian experience. King David had to learn the hard way that restoration is part of God's plan. Let us therefore bounce back when we do sin. By all means fight against sin with every ounce of spiritual energy, but when you do sin, remember the reality of 1 John 2:1,2, 'If anybody does sin, we have one who speaks to the Father in our defence – Jesus Christ, the Righteous One. He is the atoning sacrifice for our sins, and not only for ours but also for the sins of the whole world.'

Our ultimate foundation is Jesus. He must take complete precedence in your life: be totally in love with him! He must be in charge of your emotions and your money and your time. As you give yourself humbly to the Lord and to your fellows, the Spirit will work in and through you. If I hadn't seen the Spirit doing this in thousands of lives over the past twenty-odd years, then I wouldn't preach about it, because I'm interested in *practical* Christian living. I can assure you that it really works.

6.

DISCIPLINES OF THE SPIRITUAL LIFE

One great weakness in today's Christian world – perhaps particularly in Britain – is that people think and learn without acting upon what they have thought and learnt. Evangelical Christians get an enormous amount of good teaching: in the UK there are more people per capita teaching the word of God than in any other country in the world, including America. British Christians have been spoiled and pampered in this respect, and I fear that a special judgment may well fall upon the British, as upon the servant who hid his talent in the ground, because of our lack of response. Northern Ireland is a particular example, for in that country there are an extraordinary number of preachers and churches and conventions. Yet all this wisdom is not getting out into the world. This is not to attack the beautiful believers of Northern Ireland, but it is still a fact that very, very few young people have gone out from there in the past years as missionaries.

Such thoughts may come as a bit of a shock. I can hear people saying, 'But how can we send anyone out? We don't have enough pastors and teachers here ourselves.' No one ever thinks they have enough teachers. Yet there have never been enough missionaries or pastors in any of the countries that I've ever lived in: in Spain there are whole provinces with only a few gospel churches. In India, in those states where the churches are responding and growing, there is such a need for Bible teachers that when

Operation Mobilisation has sent in mechanics, who perhaps couldn't even give their testimonies properly, they have been asked to become Bible teachers – and I get letters saying that they are now teaching the Word of God among the believers.

I have been in churches in Britain where they have had six or eight trained men capable of teaching, yet were not doing so. Maybe they were comparing themselves to one of the outstanding men such as John Stott or Alan Redpath, but there is no point in making comparisons of this kind. The world will not be won for Christ simply through the ministry of a few men especially anointed by God. Such men should be ministering to the ministers!

In the West, we have sermons and Bible teaching from the pulpit, in books, on radio and cassette. Yet in many lands a modern version of the Bible is not available, and there are still over 3000 languages across the world into which no part of the Bible is translated. This is where the great work of the Wycliffe Bible Translators comes in. I believe that encouraging workers to go overseas will actually strength the Christian ministry in the West: others will get trained up to fill the gaps, and a church with a vision for missions overseas will usually find a vision for missions at home. We don't want to neglect the work at home, but to encourage both.

If we are going to take advantage of our own wealth of teaching then we must learn to lead a disciplined life. When people talk about discipline they mean as a rule fasting, and regular Bible study and prayer, and perhaps confession. These things are good and should be a part of every Christian's life, and I would strongly recommend a book entitled *Celebration of Discipline* by Richard J Foster which discusses the use of these disciplines in some detail. But I want to encourage you to think of discipline as an attitude towards the whole of your life. Even the bleakest of moments can be occasions for learning and profit. If you can learn to look for hidden riches and good results during times of challenge and anguish, then you will find that it is a matter of real fact rather than of pious conviction that the

Lord is truly in control. This will lead to reality in your prayer and witness, and to power in your service.

The author of the letter to the Hebrews refers to this truth in 12:7–12. 'Endure hardship as discipline; God is treating you as sons. For what son is not disciplined by his father? If you are not disciplined (and everyone undergoes discipline), then you are illegitimate children and not true sons. Moreover, we have all had human fathers who disciplined us and we respected them for it. How much more should we submit to the Father of our spirits and live! Our fathers disciplined us for a little while as they thought best; but God disciplines us for our good, that we may share in his holiness. No discipline seems pleasant at the time, but painful. Later on, however, it produces a harvest of righteousness and peace for those who have been trained by it. Therefore, strengthen your feeble arms and weak knees!'

What are these disciplines?

Firstly, the *discipline of disappointment*. God can use disappointment very wonderfully: he has the sovereign ability to use everything that comes into our life. This is not to say that God *sends* everything into our life: that would be to adopt a very masochist theology. We should distinguish between God's permissive will and God's perfect will, between what God allows to happen to us in our fallen world and what God actually wishes to happen to us. We should remember that many of the things that happen to us are the direct result of man's sin. Yet God can use everything. If disappointment comes to us, we should remember that we have not yet resisted sin to 'the point of shedding your blood' (Hebrews 12:4). Put all suffering in this perspective. Suffering can be a most valuable means to chasten and discipline us and bring us back to the Lord. Those who suffer rarely find it a real barrier to faith: it is the idea of suffering that causes problems.

Perhaps you look at those who are Christian leaders, with a seemingly successful spiritual life and a wide public ministry, and feel jealous. That is a big mistake. No one with my kind of personality and with as many goals, burdens, visions and ideas, is likely to be free of disappointment for long, and I have had my full share. There are people who have professed conversion and have now fallen away, and I am in correspondence with many of these. One brother came to work with us in Europe for a year, and was very dear to us. But we did not recognise the depth of a social problem he was facing, and at the end of that year he went right away from the Lord. Another young man was a stalwart in the faith for many years, but then turned away completely. He came from a very bad home background, and he went right back to his old ways. If you are going to get involved with people – and Christians must be deeply involved, in order to love in truth – then you will be disappointed. Yet this is a chance for you to recognise that you must turn the problem over to God, and to trust that his timing and planning is correct. Remember, through whatever period of darkness that you have to struggle, that God is there and that he will never leave you nor forsake you. Eventually the light will break upon you.

I recognise that this is not an easy issue. I deal with it in greater detail in a later chapter entitled 'Discouragement', so do turn to that now if you want to.

Then there is the *discipline of danger*. It often worries me that the average evangelical Christian does everything he can to avoid danger. But to be a Christian is precisely to be exposed to danger. I can hear you saying, 'But what danger is there here, in America or Western Europe? You only meet danger if you paddle up the Amazon or go out as a missionary.'

It is a great mistake to put missionaries on a special pedestal. I have met adulterers, fornicators, liars, embezzlers on the mission field. If this surprises you, read your New Testament. Missionaries are real people, with real problems. This is why we should be holding missionary prayer meetings and agonising over the condition of our missionaries. I have heard of missionaries who have gone out to India to witness for Jesus and have ended up by becoming Hindus or Buddhists themselves. Pray for them indeed: we have sent them into danger. And praise God for the majority of missionaries who serve God faithfully!

Do not think, however, that the only danger we will meet at home is the preacher going on too long with his sermon. We are at war. We are exposed and vulnerable and Satan is on the attack. If you read your Bible you will see that those who love the Lord are constantly exposed to danger. Yet danger is not something to be avoided, any more than it is something to be sought in foolishness; it will come as we move obediently forward against Satan's territory. I do not refer simply to spiritual danger. Many of our cities are becoming more and more dangerous in ordinary physical terms, and sadly there are not many Christians who are willing to go into these areas, for fear that they may be attacked. We have little holy islands in the city, little corner churches, but no one is deceived. We are at war, and everyone who reads this book is either a missionary or a mission field. (Many of us feel we are both.) As the Spirit begins to move he will send us into danger.

This reluctance to get stuck in is false caution. It is perfectly possible to face danger and death in the nicest places. One friend of mine lived in a very pleasant suburb with no obvious dangers; yet his small son was electrocuted in the garden of his house through an overlooked loose wire. Thousands die from car accidents each year. Children get into the medicine cabinet and drink poison. Many are willing to face danger for money: see how many flock for jobs on the North Sea oil rigs for the high wages paid there. It is far better to be willing to face danger – whether it is a knife in some city alley or the scorn of your workmates – for the sake of the gospel. For Jesus, however, most of us seem to want a no-risk programme, and it is very sad.

The right response to danger is daring: the *discipline of daring*. There is a story of two daring men in Numbers 13. The majority of the Israelites were afraid to enter the Promised Land, as the walls were too high, the enemy too numerous, the champions too strong. But there were two faithful scouts, Caleb and Joshua, and in verse 30 we find that 'Caleb silenced the people before Moses and said, "We should go up and take possession of the land, for we can certainly do it."' If we are not willing to dare we will not enter the Promised Land either, or at least we will never know Promised Land living, victorious living. CT Studd said, 'God is not looking for nibblers of the possible, but for grabbers of the impossible.' We must be as willing as Caleb to dare, to gamble and trust. You just cannot read the Old or the New Testament without coming across men who were gamblers for God.

Do not get the idea that I am a courageous daredevil for God, ready to go anywhere. Far from it. Down inside me is a deep, deep fear of the unknown. But I do believe that the Spirit of God produces courage in the life of the believer. This is, however, an experience that few of us have had, because so much of our evangelical faith today is little more than words. We have never been truly tested. We think that we are sanctified, that we are ready to go all out for God, but we simply haven't yet had to face the music. I do know for sure that I wouldn't have got anywhere at all in the Christian life if I hadn't been prepared to gamble, to say to the Lord, 'Well, I haven't got much faith, and I'm not very strong, and I don't know much, but. . . I'll go. I believe that somehow you'll hold it together.'

We nearly *shook* with fear when we realised the dangers of the ship* project – an old vessel, no insurance, all those young people aboard with their parents hovering anxiously in the background. I used to have nightmares about the ship going down, and would wake up thinking, 'Let's keep it in the warmer climates, so that if it does sink at least the kids will have a chance. If you go down in cold seas there's far less hope.' Yet time and time again the word of God has pulled me out of these fears and thrust me again into times of courage, especially the book of Joshua. It would be worth while memorising the following passage from chapter one where the Lord commissions Joshua to lead the people of Israel into the Promised Land after the death of Moses.

'Be strong and courageous, because you will lead these people to inherit the land I swore to their forefathers to give

* m.v. *Logos* (see note on p.23).

them. Be strong and very courageous. Be careful to obey all the law my servant Moses gave you; do not turn from it to the right or to the left, that you may be successful wherever you go. Do not let this Book of the Law depart from your mouth; meditate on it day and night, so that you may be careful to do everything written in it. Then you will be prosperous and successful. Have I not commanded you? Be strong and courageous. Do not be terrified; do not be discouraged, for the Lord your God will be with you wherever you go.' (Joshua 1:7,8)

Joshua could well have felt nervous! Like him, one of the ways in which we can become more courageous is by meditating on the word of God day and night.

Many young people and many adults too shy away from the thought of going to the mission field for fear that they will not make it. What sort of Christianity do we have in our bellies that we turn away from the mission field in such fear? What about all the promises to be found in the Bible, such as those made to Joshua? The Christian church, for all its supposed emphasis on the laity, is in fact becoming more and more professional. There are more and more people today in the church who do what they are doing, whether they would admit it or not, because they are getting paid. There's a lot of unemployment about! Once I heard a man giving a superb, most powerful sermon. I was very moved – so much so that during it I rededicated my life. I went up to him at the end of the service, and as I was waiting to speak to him I looked around at all the church people with their expensive suits and new cars. I asked him whether he really thought they would respond (I was about nineteen at the time). Then I noticed that he too was very well dressed. He looked down at me and said, 'See here, young man, I'm an evangelist, and this is my living. This is how I make my money, by preaching and doing God's work. What I was speaking about, that was all true, but I doubt if anyone would really live that way, unless perhaps there was a war on.' I walked away feeling very shaken.

Please do not misunderstand me. I do not object to ministers and other 'full-time' Christian workers (for in one sense we must all be full-time Christians) receiving their due reward: indeed, we often pay them far too little. Parish priests in England are some of the lowest-paid workers in the country. But I tell that anecdote to illustrate how far professionalism can take hold. The Christian faith is far too important to be left in the hands of the professionals. No one can afford to sit back. Moreover, to create and pay a class of professionals is bad stewardship. How can it be that Christians in some countries can earn so many thousands of pounds while evangelists and pastors in other parts of the world cannot afford a bicycle to visit the thousands of people to whom they are taking the word of God? How inconsistent can you get?

There are so many comfortable, biblical, middle-class evangelical churches where, because we do not wish to judge or pry we are secure from one another. This is well, for if we were to ask awkward questions we should begin to wonder why we all have the same standard of living, like a flock of well-dressed sheep. I am not saying that all who live this way are lost: simply that they have not appreciated their inconsistency in this area. It takes a very radical and brave person to see his own faults.

Once again, it all comes down to the discipline of daring, of being willing to take risks for God. This is what the life of faith is, by definition. We are so security-conscious. We take out fat insurance policies. We save for retirement. Where is the verse of Scripture that says we should have a nest-egg laid up? Is there nothing we can leave in the hands of God? Must everything be left in the paws of the government or the insurance companies? In gold bricks underneath the bed? We are so controlled, so prudent. I know of course of the comforting horror stories, like the one about the young man who went out trusting God and ended up in a ditch eating apples. May I say that I have never found anyone in this category, though I have heard such stories repeatedly used as a justification for keeping things as they are. I *have* heard many missionaries and others praising God for his generous provision.

Are you willing to be under attack, like Caleb and

Joshua, to risk danger? This attitude of daring and trust can pervade our whole lives, make our faith a thing of joy and excitement in every little decision we make, as well as the great ones.

There is indeed danger, especially in reaching out to new lands, and I doubt if a summer goes by without one of the members of Operation Mobilisation finding themselves in prison. This should not be a surprise. In the Book of Acts Paul and his companions were constantly in and out of prison. Yet today when the big Bible teacher comes to speak he checks into the local Hilton at £60.00 per night. When Paul was going to a town he would send one of his companions to check out the local jail! Read 2 Corinthians 11:23–29.

Then comes the *discipline of the declining days*. I believe that one of the very subtle attacks of Satan is to get people lonely, discouraged and confused during their period of senior citizenship. One of the great strengths and encouragements to me has been to see my father and mother, who are now seventy or more, and who came to Christ during their late forties, serving the Lord quietly and persistently in their own way during what people call the declining years. There is no reason why, despite physical infirmity, you should not know and experience life richly, and age can be a great discipline, concentrating the mind on the things that are truly important. Discipline in one area often breeds discipline and brings reward in another, and it takes discipline to run the race to the end – or at least walk to the end. Often the most valuable praying is done by the elderly. It's a great mistake if we think the world is going to be evangelised by youth movements.

I frequently have to take myself to task for neglecting the *discipline of delay*. Impatience is one of my greatest failings, and God has dealt with it to some extent by means of delay. He taught me to wait for six long years while the m.v. *Logos* project got off the ground. I find myself constantly irritated by long waits for planes and trains and people. Yet God can use this: I believe that he often allows delay as a means of taking us deeper into himself. Quite often our prayers fail to take account of the timing: we become concerned that the Lord is not answering us, but in fact our prayers are bang on target – simply our estimation of the timing is wrong.

One particular area where we need to learn God's patience is in the question of finding a husband or wife. There are quite a number of men and women in the churches who are still waiting, and this can be the cause of a good deal of pain. Some have had to wait until they were thirty-five or forty before God brought along the right man or woman. Many marriages get rushed into, and end in disaster. Do not be unduly super-spiritual, since there is a strong need for common sense, particularly in this sensitive area. Do realise, however, that you are men and women under God's authority, like the centurion (Luke 7:8), and that patient obedience is a good teacher. 'The testing of your faith develops perseverance. Perseverance must finish its work so that you may be mature and complete, not lacking anything' (James 1:3,4).

Try also to cultivate in yourself the *discipline of dependability*. David was faithful in a small matter – he looked after a few sheep conscientiously – and from these small beginnings he became one of the greatest leaders this world has known. One part of dependability is accuracy, a desire to do things properly, and David was a master on the harp. Not for him the half-hearted attitude which so many adopt when they buy a guitar, strumming a few chords and giving it up. He became so competent upon the harp that it led him to the palace of the king.

Dependability is a rare virtue. It is simply amazing how often you ask someone to do something and it just doesn't get done. Dependability does not come through an emotional commitment at some meeting or through reading a book: it comes rather by the daily discipline of self, the day-in-day-out denial of self in the service of Jesus.

Another part of dependability is detail. One small mistake can lead to an awful lot of tragedy. One of the things that we try to teach in OM is how to get organised – addresses, papers, time. Christians are working to contact others for Christ; make sure you keep phone numbers of those you speak to. I have known of people saved because of a single phone call or letter. A few seconds of spiritual laziness can trip you up. We are in the spiritual Olympics, where the stakes are far higher than sporting honour: we are going after the souls of men. Detail is very important in working for God's glory – but we must, as we consider this realm of our service, also remember the rest of faith, doing the best we can and then letting go and leaving the problems to God. Please do not make of this a big stick to beat yourself with. Jesus died to set you free from guilt.

I would especially encourage you to take to yourself the *discipline of discipling men*. Look at Paul's instructions to Timothy in 2 Timothy 2:1,2, 'You then, my son, be strong in the grace that is in Christ Jesus. And the things you have heard me say in the presence of many witnesses entrust to reliable men who will also be qualified to teach others.' This was the method Jesus used – man to man evangelism, one person encouraging and teaching another. This is more expensive in terms of time, but it is infinitely more effective than simply lending one another books or inviting one another along to meetings. Christians have a real duty to encourage one another, personally, taking time to explore subjects together and to learn together how to rely on God. It is a strategy which Operation Mobilisation adopted many years ago when the movement was just getting under way, and we have found no reason to change it.

Yet discipling is a sadly neglected ministry. We seem to manage to read the gospels without seeing the basic pattern of Christ's education of his disciples. Out he would go into the towns and villages, healing and teaching, and using opportunities as they arose to offer his pupils some new insight. If Christ the Rabbi, the master teacher, could use this system, then it is not for us to neglect it. We throw out messages, we get masses of people flocking to conventions and seminars, but while they do retain some benefit they remember much less than they should. I am convinced that they would do far better if they got regular encouragement in their own churches, especially if each church made fuller

71

use of talented and informed members within its own ranks to teach the newer and less well instructed.

Many of the young people who come on summer missions with Operation Mobilisation have never done any evangelism before. They need to be taken by the hand and shown how. Most of us are not very good at learning such things from books. What is true of evangelism is equally true of pastoral counselling, youth work, leading Bible studies, you name it. By contrast it seems to me that in most churches the poor pastor has the task of teaching the whole congregation, with all its widely varying needs and fears and ambitions. Any educationalist would tell you that the smaller the ratio of pupils to teachers the better. In consequence half the congregation knows the subject well, the other half is struggling to keep up.

The biblical principle is very different. While there was (and is) a place for the mass meeting, Paul and his companions were careful to place the responsibility for the oversight of each new congregation in the hands of responsible elders, with the injunction that the chain of teaching should go on from man to man, as we saw in the extract above from 2 Timothy. The leaders disciple others, who in turn disciple others, right down to the grass roots of the congregation – who as they reach out are in their turn discipling outside the church on an individual grass roots basis, by far the most effective means of spreading the gospel. Jesus did not simply give out a set of instructions: instead he lived with his disciples, caring, suffering, talking, illustrating from their common life along the road. In our churches today, the modern equivalent is for the pastor to be training the leaders, who then train others.

Perhaps you feel this is all quite unrealistic. You are completely incapable of training anyone else: it would be like a fish showing people how to ride a bicycle. Remember that the best way of learning something is to teach it. As you try to explain sticky passages and wrestle with awkward questions, the word of God will become more and more real to you – and it will give you a real impetus to find things out, asking those older than you in the faith and digging into commentaries. Just think what would happen if you could, in the next six months, disciple just one other person, and then in the following six months you could both disciple one other person each, and so on – how the word would spread! Perhaps it seems modest to you as a goal, but such a progression soon mounts up. All too frequently Christians in aiming at the stars don't even hit the trees. We become number neurotics. How many people were there at that meeting? A thousand? Praise the Lord! Yet God is more concerned with quality. (And beware also, for those on the front line get attacked. Satan will do all he can to put his oar in when he sees people being won to the Lord: and when he manages to draw any one disciple he will rejoice, because that whole congregation of believers that might have been reached through that one person may now be cut off.)

A further discipline, a further practice which I would urge you to adopt is what I call the *discipline of distribution* – the distribution of Christian literature. I used to feel faintly embarrassed at taking up good preaching time talking about Christian books, but recently I found moral support from no less a person than John Wesley. Wesley said that the Methodist faith would die out in a generation if the Methodists were not a reading people. He told his preachers that it was necessary for them to spend at least five hours in every twenty-four reading, warning them that one could never be a good preacher without extensive reading, any more than a thorough Christian. He aimed at the education of his followers by editing and publishing some of the great Christian classics. Every preacher was expected to distribute his books, the content of which he expected them to master. Wesley was criticised for pushing his wares from pulpit and platform, but he would not be put off, for he believed that his ministry in print was as important as his preaching. To his preachers he said, 'Exert yourselves in this, be not weary, leave no stone unturned, as a travelling preacher is a book steward.' The Methodist Conference of the day exhorted them to be more active in distributing books.

Ordinary Christians can and should be more active in distributing Christian literature, including magazines and cassettes. You can take Christian papers from door to door. You can put Christian magazines in waiting rooms and surgeries. One of the most effective means of evangelism at the moment is the small house meetings for those who wouldn't go to a church or to a specifically religious gathering. At such times you can have a display of Christian books, and during coffee and biscuits you can explain a little about some of the titles on the stall and perhaps ask someone to talk about how one particular book has affected him or her. It is amazing how good a salesman you can become if you get excited about something! Just look at Tupperware parties and how successful they are: Christian book parties can be just as effective. The vast majority of the people are not in the churches, so we have to go out to where they are, and make contact. Yet it does take discipline. Tract distribution is especially hard, but can be immensely valuable. You can engage in 'spontaneous' distribution by always having some tracts in your pocket and passing them to people on planes, trains, buses – even to the man on the petrol pump. Do you ever leave a tract for your milkman? There are unlimited opportunities if you are prepared to take the initiative.

In the last chapter I discussed the place doubt plays in the Christian life. I should like to make it clear that there is a *discipline of doubt*. You will remember that I suggested that it is quite normal to doubt, and that doubts will come to anyone who has a brain. Please do not do as so many young people feel they should, who get so ashamed of their doubts (as if they indicated a weak and vacillating spirit, rather than an honest mind) that they are unwilling to ask questions, instead suppressing them and all clear thinking at the same time. As a result, when they are discussing matters with a non-Christian and get asked a question they can't answer, they do not come back and say, 'I don't know, but I'll see if I can find out.' Rather they reply airily, 'Well, you have to take these things on faith, brother,' and go on to quote John 3:16 and a few other verses they have learnt out of context. Away walks the poor non-Christian in disgust.

It is, rather, a sign of a healthy mental and spiritual state, to doubt when there are so many strange and terrible things happening around the world and so much muddled thinking and wrongheadedness in the churches. But do not hide behind your doubts: use them. Ask questions. Learn to live in faith when you have not yet found a solution to a given problem, for it is amazing how many problems fade away to nothing with a little more time and a cooler brain to consider them. You can glorify Christ in the midst of doubt, living with unreconciled tension and still placing your trust in him. Your faith will be a great deal stronger if you have fought and won than if you have known no conflicts. The Christian who knows no conflicts is ducking the issue, however: if you finish this book determined to be a really valiant soldier of Christ, you will certainly find some fiery darts coming in your direction. Doubt can be a strengthener, but it can be a loophole for Satan if you let it fester.

Doubts change with circumstance. You may have never wondered before whether the 'heathen' are truly lost. It is fairly easy to say with certainty that the drunk down the road, who curses whenever Christ's name is mentioned and has spurned him time and again, is not a Christian; it is a different matter to consider the people of China or North India, who have never heard of the gospel, and to ask whether they too are lost. If you end up witnessing in a Hindu or Muslim country, you will discover a whole range of intellectual questions that you have never had to face before. The same applies if the Lord gives you a burden for Muslims in your own country. New initiatives will often produce new tests of faith that you have to battle through.

Having said all of this, and having acknowledged that there are good intellectual grounds for faith, and that some of the world's finest scientists are Christians, we must still recognise that there are some questions without answers. They are usually questions at a philosophical rather than a practical level: the origins of the soul, the relationship between predestination and freewill, the suffering caused by natural disaster. In such instances all we can say finally is that, with St Paul, we 'see through a glass, darkly'.

Sometimes I am assailed by great waves of doubt. I think that Jesus Christ was just a man, that it is possible for great masses of people to be deceived, for the whole church down the ages to have been mistaken. At such times I have to battle hard to a place of faith, even though I recognise in such thoughts the prevailing corrosive cynicism of the West. One of the things that helps me is to keep it simple. It is best to put the church and the evangelical doctrines, and all the rest to one side, and to simply ask, 'Is there a God?' I have never been able to get round the fact that if I deny the existence of God I create for myself far more intellectual, and emotional, problems than if I allow that God exists. The order of the universe points to a creating intelligence. Every human society has given a prominent place to some form of religion: even today in the so-called godless West, every popular newspaper carries a horoscope, and tales of the supernatural fill every bookstall. The arguments are many. What explanation will you choose for the acts of Jesus, for the rapid growth of the church despite persecution? As you wrestle with such questions and contemplate a bleak and godless universe without meaning or purpose, where the tenderest human love is race perpetuation or herd instinct, you find for yourself that doubt is truly a beneficial discipline, for it drives you back to the centre of all things. Once God's existence is accepted, I soon find my mind able to believe the other basic doctrines of my biblical faith.

I associate with doubt the *discipline of disillusionment*, for it too drives you back to God, and it is just as common. I have been disillusioned many times, as have we all, with some person or church in whom we place the highest confidence, only to find our trust misplaced and crumbling in confusion and hurt feelings. You find those who come along talking big, full of great ideas, and then things go wrong, turn sour, financial questions raise their heads and the end is worse than the beginning. Disillusionment then comes upon you like a plague. The discipline comes in your reaction to it.

Consider the story of Joseph, disillusioned with his own brothers. He must have felt so hurt, bouncing up as he did with all his dreams of how they would all bow down to him, all young and excited. 'I didn't mean any harm,' you can hear him crying as they push him into the cistern. Yet Joseph had his own maturity, and saw in these events the hand of God at work. Rather than wallowing in the injustice of it all, he clung to the insight right through the years in an Egyptian dungeon. Looking beyond the immediate pain, he was able to be the channel of salvation for the whole country. This is so often the Christian path. The bloody, disastrous war in Bangladesh turned out to be the opportunity for the greatest advance of the gospel that land has ever known. God is sovereign over all the states of man, even over man's sin – though that doesn't mean that when we see God overruling that we have been given a retrospective licence for having sinned!

It is amazing how God can turn a sow's ear into a silk purse. You can marry the wrong person and God can still work it out. If you think that there is only one girl for you to marry, then your God lives in a matchbox. God is great. He can make a go of your mistakes. That does not mean that you should put this book down and go and marry the first good-looking girl that walks down the street. The point to remember is that even in the midst of pain we should keep in mind that he is in control.

During our lives most of us will be disillusioned with our marriage partners or our closest friends, with our parents or our children; leaders with followers, followers with leaders. We are not good at building long-term, lasting relationships that hold when the wind's blowing. In the churches people seem to shift around like pieces on a gigantic chess board. I am convinced that God wants us to stay in unity and build close bonds with one another, not asking the impossible of our fallible friends but staying faithful. Otherwise, what do you get? A steady increase in broken relationships, hard feelings, bitterness. An enormous number of missionaries have come home from the field because of poor relationships: it is probably the biggest single cause of failure on the mission field, despite the fact that the Christian faith is a religion of love. We Christians preach a lot about forgiveness, but we are very poor at practising it. Yet forgiveness is one of the principle antidotes for disillusionment.

Do not nurse your hurt feelings. You may be confused and upset when you see Christians snapping and snarling at one another, each insisting that their religious practices or doctrines are the right ones. Reach out instead in gentleness of spirit, knowing that the Lord works with the material to hand. Does your own church have no weaknesses? Of course it does – it is full of people like you! Yet the kind of super-idealism that characterises so many evangelicals makes them unwilling to see that the Lord can use many different means of worship and church administration to serve his ends. Very little in church history has been pure truth. Happily the Lord does *not* say, 'I will only accept you after you have got all your doctrines right and your church practices word perfect!'

Fight too against disillusionment with yourself, and seek to accept your own humanity. It has been a great struggle for me to accept that I'm not as flexible as I would like to be, and sometimes believe myself to be. Although I've lived in Britain for the past twenty years, and more, I still think like an American, speak quasi-American, and my favourite food is a hotdog, a hamburger and a milkshake. I like to think of myself as an extrovert, able to get along with everyone, but I always find it hard to be amongst a great crowd of people, and unfortunately much of my life has been spent in shared accommodation. Often we think of ourselves as able in Christ's strength to love all men, but there are always a few people who really bring a sour taste to our mouth. It is unrealistic to pretend that such tendencies don't exist. Do not think that because you have such reactions the Holy Spirit cannot work in you and through you: that is a sure path to cynicism and depression. Sometimes when people stand up after a meeting to dedicate themselves to the Lord's service, I have to tell them to go away and sit down and accept themselves first. Understand that although the Spirit is within you, you still have to let off steam from time to time.

Face disappointment, disillusionment, delay, the declining years and realise that they are part of God's means to encourage you to reach out for greater faith and greater compassion, greater reality. Face danger with joyful daring. Use your doubts. Cultivate dependability, that you may disciple men more effectively. Distribute good Christian literature of all kinds, carefully suiting the book or the tract to the man. Acknowledge God's timing, and cultivate patience. Above all, keep in mind that God knows all about us, and knows our lack of discipline and loves us just the same. You don't gain any merit with God by being disciplined: there is nothing to be gained by developing an interesting neurosis on the subject. Your motivation and reward are God's mercy and love.

7.

WEAPONS AND WARFARE

'Fallen man has created a perpetual crisis. Until Christ reigns over a new, redeemed, restored world, the earth remains a disaster area,' wrote A W Tozer. I do not think anyone with a biblical faith would seriously contest this: everywhere the evil things man does are blazoned across newspaper headlines. Even now in a dozen different places around the world, people are being murdered, tortured and killed in the name of God. Our Lord must weep afresh at the atrocities committed in his name. Sometimes we get so sick that we can take no more, and turn off the radio and avoid the papers: but then some fresh thing occurs to remind us of the evil in men's hearts, perhaps within our own family. The point of these bleak reflections is that we will get a lot further, faster, if we recognise and take to heart the fact that Satan has made rack and ruin of this good earth.

Let us look too at the extent of the task. We may feel that the churches are growing strongly in many parts of the world, and so indeed they are, but experts in the field of population movement and growth estimate that the world population will *double* in the next forty years. One million or more are added every month. Probably one in twenty-five of all human beings who have ever lived are alive today.

With these facts in mind it is not surprising that at least half the people in the world have never heard the gospel. Some missionary magazines and books rather leave one with the impression that worldwide evangelisation is only a matter of time. More careful research will show that in densely populated areas the work of evangelism is going backwards rather than forwards. Giving a man a gospel tract is hardly evangelising him in the full sense of the word, but even by this poor definition less than half the world has had this bare minimum witness.

In view of this our tactics are simply crazy. Perhaps 80 per cent of our efforts for Christ, weak as they often are, are still aimed at only 20 per cent of the world's population. Literally hundreds of millions of dollars are poured into every kind of Christian project at home, especially buildings, while a thin trickle goes out to the 'regions beyond'. Half-hearted saints feel that by giving just a few hundred pounds they have done their share. I am not keen to criticise the efforts of any group that is getting the gospel out, but if we are going to be realistic we must pray and work towards stepping up the intensity and purity of the present campaign tenfold. Often the very people doing the job do not have a really deep commitment to the Lord. We have all measured ourselves so long by the man next to us that we can barely see the standard set by men like Paul, or by Jesus himself.

During the Second World War the British showed themselves capable of astonishing sacrifices (as did many other nations). They lived on meagre, poor rations. They cut down their railings and sent them for weapons manufacture. They lived in the most abstemious conditions. Yet today, in what is more truly a World War, Christians live as peacetime soldiers. Look at Paul's injunctions to Timothy in 2 Timothy 2:3,4 'Endure hardship with us like a good soldier of Christ Jesus. No-one serving as a soldier gets involved in civilian affairs – he wants to please his commanding officer.' We seem to have a strange idea of Christian service. We will buy books, travel miles to hear a speaker on blessing, pay large sums to listen to a group singing the latest Christian songs, but we forget that we are soldiers.

Imagine what would happen if someone were to explode a bomb in your street tonight. Phone calls would go out for doctors and police, others would be providing hot water and bandages, sheltering the wounded, searching for further 'devices'. Anyone not helping as they could would be branded as a traitor: a man without compassion. *Satan has exploded bombs today in every town and village in the land.* Any Christian who is not on the job, rescuing people, is a traitor to the cause of Jesus Christ, no matter what doctrinal banner he may carry.

We do not go empty-handed into battle, for the Lord has given us weapons. 'The weapons we fight with are not the weapons of the world. On the contrary, they have divine power to demolish strongholds. We demolish arguments and every pretension that sets itself up against the knowledge of God, and we take captive every thought to make it obedient to Christ' (2 Corinthians 10:4,5). We exercise these weapons on two fronts, the inner war against temptation, doubt, cynicism, and the outer war against the activity of Satan in circumstances and in those we meet, wherever his strongholds may be.

Some of the weapons are listed in that well-loved jewel of a passage, Ephesians 6:10–18. This is one of the sections of the Bible that it is imperative to Christians to have by heart, not least because the sword of the Spirit, with which we advance to attack, is the word of God itself. I have considerable difficulty in memorising Scripture, but take heart from the story of the man who tried to carry water home from the river in a wicker basket. By the time he had climbed half way up the hill, the basket was empty: he filled it afresh, but the same thing happened again. An onlooker queried the wisdom of the action, and he replied, 'No, I don't collect much water, but my basket gets a little cleaner each time.' Scripture memorisation is also a valuable mental discipline. It is by the word, as we saw when considering the foundations for spiritual growth, that we are fed and grow as Christians. But we must feed ourselves, not endlessly spooning in pap, but disciplining ourselves to chew and digest the real meat of truth. I am in danger of mixing my metaphors here, but the point is clear: the Bible is the source of our knowledge, and the guideline by which we judge good conduct; it is the very word of God which has a unique authority in evangelism and pastoral care; it is the best possible refutation of Satan's lies. However, we must seek to keep our sword sharp, ensuring that it is a part of our daily lives and making full use of good commentaries.

With the sword of the Spirit comes the shield of faith, without which none of the teaching this book offers will become real. All these injunctions must be 'mixed with faith', or our sense of weakness and inadequacy must overwhelm us. The long record of heroes of faith in Hebrews 11, I believe, is there precisely so that we may know how much God values faith. The Bible is full of examples: Joshua taking Jericho, Moses on the mountain with his arms raised against the Amalekites. Stories of faith and victory are endless. Perhaps our palates are jaded, perhaps we have heard this kind of exhortation too often for it to have any effect. Perhaps long disobedience has ingrained the habit of listening without doing so that we are no longer able to obey. There has to be some explanation for why these many examples do not penetrate our hearts – yet if we allowed them to enter, we should become men and women of power, able to tear down the strongholds of the enemy. Our faith is not blind: God has been faithful, is faithful, so he will be faithful.

Worship and praise are other great weapons. Often when we feel the enemy moving within us we can stand against him through praise. When depression or discouragement nags at you, or you feel spiritually dry, the answer often is to praise the Lord, to thank him for what he has done for you and given you, for who he is, for the magnificence of his creation, for the authority of his word. For each of us the emphasis will be different. As we acknowledge the Lord's authority over even the dark passages in our lives, we find a new and healthier perspective. (I am not suggesting this as the only therapy, especially when clinical depression or deep wounds are concerned: but it is astonishing how often it helps.)

Make time each day just to worship the Lord, for I believe that the highest goal for every believer is not evangelism, but worship. See that it becomes your number one priority. You will find that evangelism and every other Christian activity is easier in consequence. Give worship pride of place above intercessory prayer, and simply enjoy God because he is God. Worship, Tozer comments, is the missing jewel of the evangelical church. If it is lacking in your life you are probably experiencing a power shortage.

Our motivation as we march into battle is love. As we saw in chapters three and four, unless we have love our Christian lives are not only dull and painful, but noisy and worthless, 'a resounding gong or a clanging cymbal'. Yet within ourselves we cannot generate the love we need, for very few of us brim over with charity. This is not a cause for guilt, however, though it may be a sign that we need to repent of the hard feelings we have harboured against one man or all men. We need rather to turn to Christ and ask him to fill us with his love. We have Christ within us – let him out! Don't pray for the Lord to be present, for he *is* present, in the person of the Holy Spirit. Thank him for his presence. Pray that he will fill you: no matter how filled you are, he can still fill you more, seeking new areas of our lives to move into. We can't take all of God at once, for it would overwhelm us: we need to pray that he will increase our capacity. He is gentle, and will give us just as much of himself as we can take. (If we can't hold very much it is because we haven't taken the lid off!) As he reveals more and more of himself to us, so we become able to love with real heart-felt concern.

This concern will spill out in all kinds of ways. People ask, 'What's different about you?' You will find yourself wanting to reach out in all kinds of ways. A crowd of people beside the road? Stop and talk to them, give them some of the literature you keep in your car. The phone rings, and it's a wrong number? 'No sir, don't hang up, this is the right number because there's something important you ought to hear.'

We have the weapons and the motivation, we have the Spirit within us, but there is no assurance that we will not be wounded in battle. Rather the reverse: if we are fighting we shall certainly be hurt. Do not let yourself be thrown by past defeats. Don't keep on fretting about things that humiliated or depressed you, or feeling guilty once the time of repentance is past. Regret can be one of the most subtle forms of self-love. We don't have to backslide, and can go to bed every night free and worshipping the Lord. There is no reason for us to stay filled with hatred or fear. Avoid phrases like 'if only . . .' which drain away your strength: some Christians have exchanged their backbones for wishbones. 'Stand firm. Let nothing move you' (1 Corinthians 15:58). If you look at men you'll be disappointed. If you worry about situations you'll get discouraged. If you think of yourself you'll get depressed. Look to Jesus, however, and you'll be able to get up and go on from victory to victory. Keep on keeping on.

War may well demand great sacrifice from the soldier on active service. If there is anything that you value more highly than your Lord, it will have to go; moreover, the Lord may be telling you that there is something about your home that needs to be sold to pay for some aspect of his work. If you have a £2000 car, perhaps it should be a £1000 car. (If you belong to Operation Mobilisation, perhaps a £100 car!) A year or so ago, someone gave me a beaten up Mini. It wasn't very good, but then I was given a second beaten up Mini. By cannibalism we now have one beaten up but serviceable Mini, which has carried us far. Cars are really a god to our society, and Christians are particularly guilty in this respect.

Many Christians are keen to travel to Israel, a kind of pilgrimage which costs several hundred pounds. Was it well spent? Often you hear the pious comment that if Christ gave so much for us, then by comparison we can give him nothing. That is frequently just what we do. I prefer the argument that if Christ gave all for us, then what can we possibly hold back? God is probably willing for you to keep your car, but what you need to do is say, 'Thank you, Lord, for the use of this car. It is yours, so please use it as you see fit.' Perhaps you should hold a commitment service. Do you have an insurance policy which would allow other people to use it? Peter said to the beggar, 'Silver and gold have I none,' but that would be an infrequent testimony today. So often we are blind to the grip material things have upon us, but as we seek to shake it off we see results. Such action will lead to spiritual revolution.

There are four kinds of action for the soldier of Christ. The first is reproduction, which is covered under the heading of discipling men. Secondly, disciplined action, and that too we have covered. The third is united action. That doesn't mean that we have to be of one mind on every point: we may be talking about divine truth, but it is transmitted through earthen vessels, and I know that anything that comes through George Verwer has quite a lot of earth attached! However, unity is essential, and the New Testament speaks of it at length and in many contexts. It is not easy, because anyone who starts living a revolutionary life in the church today is going to find himself out of step with a lot of people. But even if we are out of step we can still exercise patience and love. If our fellowship is marred by back-biting and irritation then it will be no fellowship at all, instead of the source of encouragement and strength and love that it can be. The same applies within marriage: you and your husband or wife should be a two-person team, working closely together, not seeking constantly to outdo the other or allowing yourselves to ignore one another for the sake of 'Christian' service.

The fourth area of action is world-wide action. The churches should be following the New Testament pattern and asking themselves, 'Whom should we be sending?' So frequently it is left to the individual missionary to sense a call from God, whereas the whole church fellowship should be functioning as a commissioning body. They should be sending out their very best people. Read Acts 11–13, and you will see how the fledgling church at Antioch received word from the Holy Spirit to set aside Paul and Barnabas for further missionary work. Paul and Barnabas? But they were the people who had founded the church – they had only been there a year – how could the group possibly survive without them? But there was no such quavering, and after fasting and prayer the church laid hands on them and sent them off. Should you be sending out your own pastor, if he can preach and teach and is walking with the Lord? Do not hang on to your best men, but seek out whom the Lord needs elsewhere. This kind of thinking would make an enormous difference to the areas being evangelised: and you would find that as you tried to look beyond your own needs, so your own needs would be met. As you prayed for mission elsewhere, mission would be happening at home.

As Christians launch out into the mission field of the whole wide world, as we start living rather than talking, as we begin to give and pray in a truly sacrificial way, as we mobilise, so there will come the counterattack. I hope that you will put this book down with a sense of calling and encouragement, but you can be sure that discouragement will follow soon enough, making you doubt your commitment and causing you to stumble. The higher you go in the Christian life, the greater your fall: it is the peril of the victorious life. This means that we must work slowly and steadily, build our foundations well, and build in unity. We are not concerned to win skirmishes or even battles, but the war.

PART III

Continuing in the Way

8.

REPENTANCE

The third section of this book is designed to provide some help for day-by-day Christian living. Christians are often willing to start the race, but all too frequently they fall by the wayside. Someone once asked D L Moody, 'Why do you go on and on about being filled with the Holy Spirit again and again and again?' Moody just looked him in the eye and answered, 'Because I leak.' May I assure you that I too am a weak and leaky Christian leader – but I have discovered where the refills are! To be filled with the Holy Spirit is the normal Christian life, in Watchman Nee's memorable phrase. As you learn to walk in the Spirit day after day you grow more teachable, and can take in some of the lessons of the New Testament. The Spirit is the provision for every believer.

First of all I should like to stress the value of repentance. Please put this book down and turn to 2 Samuel 11 and 12, and remind yourself of the story of David, Bathsheba, Uriah and Nathan. The sins that David committed were several: adultery, murder, dishonesty, self-deception, faithlessness in return for faithful service. His crime was not a momentary lapse, but a long-term refusal to acknowledge that he had done wrong and was doing wrong. How could he be the leader of God's chosen people under such conditions? The Golden King, the figurehead and joy of his people, had shown conclusively that he had feet of clay.

Nathan loved his king, but he loved his Lord more, and

spoke the words the Lord gave him without caring for possible reprisals. He phrased his accusation so cleverly that David was condemned out of his own mouth, and happily retained enough integrity to admit that his sins had found him out. His repentance took just six words: 'I have sinned against the Lord.'

These six words can revolutionise the life of any believer. David was rewarded with no lengthy sermon, simply with Nathan's assurance, 'The Lord has taken away your sin. You are not going to die.' The mercy of God was, and is, ready to burst through like a thunderclap. One reason that so many Christians today are living defeated lives is that they have not recognised the truth of instant forgiveness. It seems to me that mercy was almost hovering over David, waiting to fall as soon as he gave the word and confessed that he had sinned. Often we feel beaten down by our failure to live and work as we should for the Lord, and horrified by our own false motivations. God does not want us to wallow in self-pity, or to make guilt-inducing resolutions and promises, but rather to let him drop his blessing upon us like a cloud. However, the blessing destined for us will be missed if we don't learn to repent, at once, more swiftly than David – not least because we have someone greater than Nathan to chide and guide us in the person of the Holy Spirit. Part of the work of the Spirit is to convict of sin.

As you progress in the Christian life, and get deeper into the ways of the Lord, you will find more and more that the Spirit shows you your sin. This is good. It is an essential part of the victorious life: without repentance and instant forgiveness you will go on struggling in self-pity and self-revulsion, and will be useless in battle, incapacitated by your own misery. The path ahead is to get down on your knees and say, 'Lord God, I have sinned against you. Have mercy on me.'

I don't believe in the victorious life. Not at all – if by that is meant the kind of life that is apparently without blemishes, full of prayer and soul-winning. Whenever I have met someone 'up there' I have gone away feeling that what they really needed was to get down and confess that they were loaded with pride. I do believe in the victorious life that is constant fellowship with God in Christ, a life of growth being continually cleansed by his blood. Have you repented of anything today? If you have lived right through today without sinning I would love to get to know you! Whoever marries you will be very fortunate. It says in 1 John 1:8, 'If we claim to be without sin, we deceive ourselves and the truth is not in us.' Very few days go by without my needing to repent of something or other. It doesn't have to be a big affair, and you need not even express your repentance verbally. Constantly during the day I have to say, 'You were right, Lord. I was wrong. Forgive me.' Usually it is not a question of some specific outward act of lust or cruelty or anger, but rather a sin of heart and mind, a willing progression from being tempted to harbouring sin.

Forgiveness doesn't mean that there won't be consequences. Nathan told David that the child Bathsheba bore to him would die. David must have felt ghastly, knowing that an innocent child would die because he had sinned. For seven days he fasted and prayed, lying upon his face, but he had to face the results of what he had done. I like this, in a way, terrible though it is, because it keeps the balance: God is merciful, but not over-indulgent, and in his wisdom he knew that if David had been let off more lightly then the lesson would not have struck home. The judgment still came. Once a boy and girl came up to me after a meeting and told me with much sorrow how they had slept together, and now had come back to the Lord. The Lord accepted them but that didn't stop the birth of the baby or the great suffering that came to them and their families as a result of what they had done.

This then is an additional reason why we should keep short accounts with God. If we do so, we shall never get into the kind of mess that David found himself in; but if we let the sins pile up and our relationship with God grow faint, then we shall regret it bitterly. I know of one Christian youth ministry that was wiped out in one city after another because members of the team sinned as David did. David should have repented upon the roof, not a year later; he reached the stage that no believer should have to reach, where he had to be called forth and publicly rebuked. Essentially he had become a hypocrite. The double life can go very deep: you can be sitting reading this book and know that you are worse off than David was, no matter what your fellow Christians may think of you.

Repentance is a key word in Scripture. The Laodicean church was guilty not of drunkenness or immorality, but of a lukewarm heart and of smug satisfaction with their material wealth. Many of us need to repent in these two areas! Look at what the Lord told them: 'I counsel you to buy from me gold refined in the fire, so that you can become rich; and white clothes to wear. . . Those whom I love I rebuke and discipline. So be earnest, and repent' (Revelation 3:18,19).

Usually repentance is a purely private affair. If your sin has injured a few, confess to those few. If your sin is a public matter, then often so should your confession be public. Frequently the hardest thing of all is to confess to your husband or wife. I remember once during the crusade in Italy in 1963 that my wife and I exchanged some particularly hard words and we went into separate rooms to lick our wounds. 'Lord,' I said, 'if she comes to me and admits she was in the wrong, I'll also apologise for what I said.' Next door she was thinking, 'Lord, if he comes in here and says he's sorry, I'll be prepared to admit that I was at fault too.' You can spend your whole life like that! I think that my wife and I are still together because neither of us has ever managed more than ten minutes in separate rooms. We've often as not bumped noses in the hall as we've run to put our arms around each other. It's the same in Christian work. When I'm under stress I get quite intolerable, nervy and silly and snappy. Many's the time I've had to phone some brother long distance to ask forgiveness. Remember, however: you may have to ask forgiveness from your marriage partner or your fellow Christian, but it is against the Lord that you have sinned, and to the Lord you must offer repentance.

Learn the secret of repentance. Then get up, go on, rejoice in God's goodness and grace and love. You're going into front line combat, and it's going to be hot and hard and sometimes you're going to want out. Remember that his mercy is available to you. Take it.

9.

DISCOURAGEMENT

By this time you will have realised that I am deeply concerned that our spiritual life should be realistic in every respect. While we should certainly be God-centred rather than problem-centred, there is little point in hiding from ourselves such problems as we do face. I have already touched on the fact that those who journey forth to war are likely to get hurt, and now I would like to specify some of the ways in which we can get hurt, so that we can be on our guard, and also some of the things that I have found helpful.

Simple, straightforward discouragement is the biggest drain on our spiritual resources. No one is free of it: many suffer from it acutely. I would reckon that at any one point perhaps 25 per cent of the personnel on the Operation Mobilisation mission teams are feeling discouraged, and they are a pretty highly motivated bunch. How much more so the pastor whose church is largely empty, or the youth club leader who has just had his clubhouse wrecked by vandals, or the young idealist who can't come to terms with his own sexuality, or the career man damaging his own prospects by remaining honest in a corrupt system? Discouragement is one of the most subtle and tricky techniques in the Devil's arsenal for stopping the forward movement of the gospel.

This is plainly visible in the great saints of the Old Testament. So often we read Christian biographies which emphasise the strong points of the man or woman of God. But as we make a detailed study of some of the Bible's characters we see discouragement plainly: Elijah after Mount Carmel, Jonah after one of the greatest evangelistic campaigns the Middle East has ever seen. In the New Testament we find that the disciples of the Lord Jesus almost specialised in saying stupid things at the wrong time: how embarrassed and confused they must often have felt as they put their foot in their mouth yet again.

Then too, those of us who yearn for higher plateaus in the things of God – who at times read perhaps too much from A W Tozer! – also get badly cast down. Why aren't God's people doing more we wonder? Why is there so much disunity? Even in Britain, which is in many ways a cynical and highly secular society, the latest statistics indicate that 11 per cent of the population goes to church, which is substantially more than those who go to football games: the church is not small. One recent speaker at Spring Harvest (the spring conference organised each year by *Buzz* and *Family* magazines) suggested that there could be as many as 100,000 cells of Christians in the UK. In the USA and many parts of Asia, Latin America and Africa the figure would be far higher, and so would the percentage of believers. In view of all this, how can we be other than discouraged at the lack of activity and the under-used potential?

I need to be careful not to make careless generalisations, as they are usually misleading. Christian leaders are very prone to simplify matters, and to say, 'We need to pray more, or to be filled with the Spirit more, or to have a greater sense of commitment.' This in itself can lead to discouragement. So I do not want to offer superficial answers, but I am pretty sure that I am correct in generalising about the overall degree of discouragement.

Discouragement breeds discouragement. You get cast down about the quality of your prayer life, so you don't get to the prayer meeting, so your pastor gets discouraged. You are ashamed of your lack of missionary zeal, so you don't attend the missionary's talk, so he gets discouraged.

The lack of reality in my own prayer life is one of the

things Satan has used to try to discourage me. Discouragement in fact attacks me almost every day: when you are thrust into the thick of spiritual warfare, and face heavy pressures on many different fronts, and attempt the impossible so frequently, you are bound to meet discouragement: it is an occupational hazard, and does not disappear as you advance in the Christian life.

In all this we badly need one another's support. If your Christian brother seems to be low on prayer power or caught up in some carnal trap or hung up on doubt, then don't shun his company: he needs love and prayer and probably quite a lot of tactful concern. It is all too easy to instil a sense of inadequacy in people. Don't judge, therefore, whether by word or attitude, but *care*. When I was at Bible college God had to take me in hand and rebuke me for my attitude towards so-called non-spiritual people, the ones who didn't show up to prayer meetings and at times made fun of spiritual things. They are often not so dead to the spiritual world as they may appear, but rather feel keenly the need to prick a few bubbles. As such they have a most valuable function. (Having a family is a good ally here: the thing that has brought more balance to my life than any book I've ever read has been having three unique, aggressive, on-the-march, ready-to-have-a-go-at-Dad offspring!)

If you are by nature an extrovert and energetic type, then do not get impatient with those of a quieter nature. Different temperaments respond to pressure in different ways. For many years I didn't understand why my wife used to get so discouraged, until I took the time to understand what her temperament, her background, her physical being were asking of her. We are all made differently, and all of us have some areas of vulnerability. Therefore do not judge.

What are some of the specific ways in which discouragement seems to attack God's people? The first, the most obvious, is through *unanswered prayer*. How are we to respond when we pray urgently, with all of our hearts, for something which is in our eyes clearly needed, and then get no response? We shrug it off, perhaps, thinking that we cannot understand all the Lord's ways, and then we hear a sermon on prayer, or read one of the more idealistic books available, and a slight cynical streak begins to develop. We are warned in Hebrews 12:15 to see that 'no bitter root grows up to cause trouble and defile many.' Cynicism is the path to bitterness, especially if you read lots of Christian biographies and find them full of miraculous answers to prayer, or if you know people who are always full of another joyful story of God's abundant grace. Now I do believe indeed that miracles happen today, even quite frequently, and that God pours out his grace upon his church to the full measure that we are able to receive. Yet unanswered – or seemingly unanswered – prayer is one of the great altars upon which God makes true men and women. My life is full of unanswered prayer. Not even 50 per cent of my prayers have been answered over the years, not yet at least. I refuse to be discouraged by this. I recently returned from a visit to Turkey, a country for which I have had a deep concern for almost twenty-five years, and there saw setback after setback in the work of OM. One of our workers in Turkey some years ago was shot by extremists on his own doorstep. I should have come out totally discouraged, yet somehow I was given the confidence to battle through in the knowledge that the Lord will do a great work in that land in his own good time. There is no harvest without sowing.

A second reason for a lot of discouragement is *failure*: in relationships, in the family, with our children. This is a common problem, and if you are worried about your family then you are not alone: the children of many Christian leaders have totally rejected Jesus. If you do have trouble in this area then you may want to pick up John White's remarkable book *Parents in Pain*. Failure may strike you as you try to witness to your faith. You hear a good series of sermons, read a book, go through a two-day training course, and launch out on your campaign of door to door evangelism, only to discover that you have tremendous difficulty relating to unconverted people. As they blow smoke in your eyes and you have a coughing fit you wonder how anyone could ever win any of these people to the Lord.

So you withdraw and decide it is better to go to the Keswick Convention for your holiday and to avoid the unsaved as much as possible. I can assure you that it is ten times as hard to witness to Muslims as to talk to someone in our own culture.

Thirdly, we get discouraged because of our own *sin*. I found that I was especially prone to discouragement in this area because I was hyper-idealistic, and for quite a long time I had false views about the victorious life. I just could not see how the victorious life could include knowing what to do when I sinned – and yet it must. The victorious Christian simply has to know what to do when he does fall, for fall he unquestionably will. Perhaps we get victory in Christ's strength over an area of particular difficulty in our life, and go for weeks or even years without failure. Then one day an unusual temptation arises when we are especially tired or depressed, and we fall in that very area. At once the accuser of the brethren is there, crying, 'Ah, you see how weak your will is – you've failed, you're finished. Your basic nature hasn't changed, you're just the same old pathetic rotten creature that you were a couple of years ago.' (The danger is of course that he is right – but remember that ours is a religion of grace.) So you get the familiar pattern which causes such depression: every summer little Johnny goes to Bible camp and recommits himself, and every winter back he slides again. Then along comes Mr Easy-Answer, one of Job's counsellors, and rams him further into despair.

Fourthly, many get discouraged because of *physical illness*. Most people don't understand this until they get ill themselves. Many illnesses have much longer-term side-effects than we realise in the forms of depression and lethargy. You and your body are one. Yet physical illness can still allow the exercise of spiritual power. I have a dear friend, a prayer partner in Bromley, whose husband, a pastor, died some while ago. She is confined to her bed and is totally deaf: I have to communicate with her by passing little notes on a pad back and forth. Yet that lady has a ministry of intercessory prayer that reaches the ends of the earth. She cannot get to church, and often is badly isolated, but she is uplifted by the presence of Jesus.

Many, fifthly, are discouraged because of the *disunity within the church*, the broken relationships, the suspicions and resentments between denominations, fellowships, and individuals. This too is the result of hyper-idealism, the kind of thinking that argues that when we get the right set of doctrines and the right spiritual blessings and the right songbooks then we shall become angels, more or less. Why have so many left the established churches and gone into house fellowships? Some have gone for legitimate reasons, but many others from a vague sense that if we get into smaller and more intimate groups and really worship the Lord properly (i.e., as he wants) then all will be well. In the process they have caused painful splits and lasting sadness. I am in touch with the leaders of many house churches, and they are going through just the same sort of battles that the big churches are going through. People are people. You put them in a church or a cathedral or a living room and they are still people, with problems. Many are now leaving the house churches as they left the main-line denominations earlier, once again discouraged and beaten down. I personally believe that because of God's love and mercy he is working in both.

The answers simply do not lie in human organisation. All too often we are seeking something in our church or house group that God has never meant to exist, and that is only found in him. The evangelical utopia doesn't exist on earth. We live on a cursed planet, filled with lost men, filled with sadness. The Christian is different not because he is immune to these things but because he is rooted and grounded in the love of God. This is our unity.

Let me outline a few basic things that we can do to stand against discouragement, remembering as we saw when examining some of the spiritual disciplines that great faith is forged as we battle through with our eyes upon the Lord.

My first practical defence is a *deeper knowledge of God himself*. I shall explore this topic more fully below. This is why I try to get people to read books by Tozer and Packer, because they have a remarkably clear understanding of our Lord. Our goal is God, and when I am much beset by problems then my first and most immediate means of relief is to turn away from Christians, who are weak and fallible, and to concentrate on the majesty, love and awesome splendour of our great Lord. It might help in doing this to turn up your favourite psalm, or perhaps David's song of praise in 2 Samuel 22.

Secondly, a *greater knowledge of God's word*. Simply spend time in the word of God. Memorise, meditate. I strongly recommend the very practical advice in this area given in Ralph Shallis's book *From Now On*.

Thirdly, stress to yourself, stress as a church that there needs to be *more emphasis on faith and less on feeling*. I am a terrible slave to my emotions: in the course of a single day I can go up and down as much as twenty-five times. If any of those who read this book lean a bit towards a similar instability then I can tell you that there is still hope: I have found it necessary to be ruthless with my feelings, to dominate my gut-level reactions. It is not easy but the reward is great.

Fourthly, constantly seek a *greater understanding of those around you*. If you are let down by someone, or meet with a lukewarm response to your excited visions for the world, then ask yourself why they are reacting like that. Perhaps they have special griefs and burdens of which you know nothing. Be a good listener, by using your imagination and calling on your reserves of sympathy, and try to believe the best about the person concerned. Your opinion of someone is often a self-fulfilling prophecy: if you expect them to react well then they may surprise themselves by doing so.

Fifthly, *keep some kind of spiritual perspective*. Try not to let the incidental encounter or calamity get you down: as you walk with God try always to see the bigger picture. If you hear a juicy titbit of gossip, refuse to respond to it in isolation. The same applies when you overhear blame or criticism heaped upon yourself, especially if you feel it was unjust – what pressure was the speaker under when he said that? I have learned not to listen to most gossip, which is a cancer on the church, but rather to believe the best and press on. We have a big God, with a big heart, and this is the reality behind the bickering church.

Sixthly, *set yourself more realistic goals*. One of the main neuroses in the USA is that Americans set extremely high goals for themselves, linked with an overemphasis on 'success', and you won't understand Americans unless you see that. Most end up either discouraged, or in pretension and hypocrisy. (Read Romans 12:3.) Keep to reasonably attainable targets in your mission work, your prayer life, your church life, unless God specifically directs you otherwise. By all means claim great things from God, but do not try to manipulate him by lofty rhetorical prayers. It is just as well the Lord has a sense of humour! I remember once in Mexico that a girl on our team started praying in a prayer meeting one night for a thousand souls to be saved. At that point hardly anyone had shown any interest. I stopped the meeting and asked, 'Did the Lord put that prayer in your heart? Because we haven't seen five yet.' Such prayer can be a covert form of boasting: 'I've got more faith than you have.'

Seventhly, *put more of an emphasis on praise and prayer*, as we discussed in the chapter on weapons. Keep your eyes on the Lord, and avoid overmuch introspection. I am involved in counselling a number of people who seem so quickly to want to put themselves down. This is not the road to humility, but to self-absorption. We are indeed unworthy servants, but we are also Spirit-filled kings, priests, friends of God. As we fix our attention upon our glorious Lord, and offer him our worship, we will know the encouragement he offers. It is God's will to work in our lives and to bless us in one way or another.

The eighth point may seem strange, but it is crucial in rising above discouragement: *Learn how to be hurt*. Unless we do so we shall participate in the general back-biting and bitterness which is a part of most church fellowships. Some people have nothing for Sunday lunch but roast pastor! You cannot hope to be effective in the Lord's service if you carry around the burden of the hurts you have been given or received for the rest of your life. Being hurt is a part of living on this planet, and forgiveness is utterly necessary. If you are being honest with yourself there is almost certainly someone against whom you feel bitter anger, and that person is probably a Christian.

For some time now I have carried around with me a little article I found called 'First Aid for Spiritual Emergency'. It has a lot of common sense, and tells you what to do when a hurt is inflicted on you by a brother or sister in Christ.

1. *Keep calm.* 'Be still, and know that I am God.' Rushing about trying to correct the injury usually causes greater damage.
2. *Apply direct pressure of understanding to the wound.* What caused the incident? Could you have prevented it? How does the offending party feel? What if things were reversed?
3. *Wash the wound thoroughly with kindness* to remove all hardness and vindictiveness.
4. *Coat liberally with the ointment of love.* This will protect from infections of resentment and bitterness.
5. *Bandage the injury with forgiveness.* This will keep it out of sight until the wound is healed.
6. *Don't take the scab off.* Bringing up the subject will re-open the wound. Serious dangers from infection (see No. 4, above) still exist which could prove fatal spiritually.
7. *Beware of painful and touchy self-pity.* This is often referred to as withdrawal pains, as the sympton is withdrawing from others, especially the one inflicting the injury. The remedy – accept apologies.
8. *Prescription.* Take a generous dose of antibiotics from the word of God several times daily, using prayer each time. This has a soothing effect and is a good painkiller.
9. *Stay in close contact with the great physician at all times.* Depend on his strength, joy and peace to help you during convalescence.

10. *Full recovery is reached* when the patient is restored to complete fellowship and harmony, especially with the offending party.

My ninth point is a wonderful antidote to discouragement, especially with yourself: *realise that God is easy to live with*. He is a God of love and mercy and forgiveness, ready to note the smallest effort. If a cup of cold water can be a deed worthy of his praise, what shall we say of witnessing, tract distribution, long-term assistance to others, faithful prayer? One of the things that has kept me going over the years has been the sureness that even at moments of utter failure he still loves me and wants me to get up and start running the race again.

Tenthly, *learn to refuel*. D L Moody was once told, 'The world has never seen a totally dedicated man.' I believe many have been led into extremes by trying to be someone they were not meant to be. The way God measures dedication, and the way Mr Fellowman measures it, are two quite different things. Since you can't achieve perfection, acknowledge the fact and give yourself some time off when you need it. For some it's a walk in the woods, or a few days' holiday, or just getting away and reading (preferably something non-spiritual). Perhaps a good film.

The Apostle Paul was a master of encouragement. He doesn't mince his hard sayings, and that makes his generous comments all the more valuable. I would like to close this chapter with one of his parting injunctions to the Corinthians, which must have been treasured by them in their tough surroundings. 'Therefore, my dear brothers, stand firm. Let nothing move you. Always give yourselves fully to the work of the Lord, because you know that your labour in the Lord is not in vain' (1 Corinthians 15:58).

10.

SPIRITUAL BALANCE

There are quite a number of areas where I believe it is important for the Christian to try to maintain balance. We have an enemy. He is not a funny little character with horns and a pitchfork, but a clever – and from the human point of view beautiful – being who is seeking to deceive and to bring havoc. We easily get into tangents and extremes if we are ignorant of his devices: not exactly getting into a cult, but developing a cult-like practice in a given area.

Once a person commits his life to Jesus, it seems that Satan does everything he can to lead him off at a tangent so that his Christian life will lose its impact. John Stott, in his excellent little book *Balanced Christianity*, points out how the Devil is concerned to polarise us and to get us into different camps, chopping away at one another rather than working together against him. This is right against the cardinal principle of love which we examined in chapter 4. Tempers rise, people grow upset and start reacting to one another in the flesh. Those who are militantly orthodox can often be unloving: it is not difficult to end up with your doctrines all correctly labelled in the right sort of packages, ready to hit your neighbour over the head! In one Bible College in England not long ago a student of Calvinistic persuasion and one with an Arminian viewpoint got so excited about their respective positions that they actually came to blows.

The first area, then, where we need to find balance is

between the crisis experience and God's growth process. Some Christians lay a heavy emphasis on crisis: they make a point of attending different conventions and house parties to find a new peak of awareness and commitment. It is easy to misuse Keswick or Filey or the Dales Bible Week or Greenbelt or even an OM conference in this way. Often such mountaintop experiences are perfectly legitimate, and we should never despise what the Spirit of the Lord may be doing – but unless that summer crisis is followed by a process it will become an abcess, generally by December, with predictable guilt and discouragement. The process of growth towards maturity is primarily your responsibility and should be taking place 365 days a year. It is not just a matter of 'let go and let God'. Love and the fruit of the Spirit are not automatic. God works in different people in different ways, for he does not destroy your individuality: as you give it to him he returns it to you, straightened and purified, made whole. Compare Colossians 3:16, 'Let the word of Christ dwell in you richly,' with Ephesians 5:18, 'Be filled with the Spirit'. We need both, and note that both are imperative. Neither is an optional extra.

We also need balance *between discipline and freedom*. Here, too, the Devil is hard at work polarising God's people, for you get those who insist on planning everything down to the very last detail, and insisting that half an hour's Quiet Time is indispensable for salvation; and then on the other side you find those who feel that such things are devilish in themselves, and a temptation to rely on the flesh rather than the Spirit. I have heard quite a number of (rather bad) sermons where the preacher felt it was unspiritual to prepare. Yet both messages are in the Bible. There is a time to step out in faith that things will work out – and sometimes we have no choice – but there is also a place for using the wits that God gave us. St Paul writes at length about freedom from the law, but can also say in 1 Corinthians 9:24–27, 'Do you not know that in a race all the runners run, but only one gets the prize? . . . Everyone who competes in the games goes into strict training. They do it to get a crown that will not last; but we do it to get a crown that will last for ever. Therefore I do not run like a man running aimlessly; I do not fight like a man beating the air. No, I beat my body and make it my slave so that after I have preached to others, I myself will not be disqualified for the prize.'

Another area is the balance *between zeal and wisdom*. Perhaps you are a young Christian, anxious to smother his neighbourhood with gospel tracts. Already you can see your elders at the church shaking their heads and muttering, 'Ah yes, we tried that in 1954, and it didn't work then. You'll only put people off.' Satan is keen to polarise the old and the young. He must rejoice when he sees churches made up almost exclusively of older people, where the only man under retiring age is the vicar – and will be quite happy too when he finds churches full of young madcaps bouncing with energy and sure that anyone who doesn't find Joe Zealot and the Fishbones the best thing since Noah has probably been around since Noah. Youngsters are often keen to condemn the established church. The Children of God called it the 'system' and encouraged people to leave it, and rebellious young people did so in great numbers. Ironically they have ended up probably more regimented than any branch of the Christian church.

The answer here lies not in moderation so much as in both extremes together: we need as much wisdom and as much zeal as we can find. We need those who can get out and get on with the job, and we also need the older and wiser members who can give counsel and help the younger ones count the cost – and press on when the first flush of enthusiasm is past. 'Never be lacking in zeal, but keep your spiritual fervour, serving the Lord' (Romans 12:11). Enthusiasm is contagious, it doesn't require much intelligence to attain it, and it is a hallmark of any flourishing church. It is one of the reasons for the enormous growth of the Pentecostal churches in Latin America.

In connection with zeal and wisdom we also need a balance *between submission and individual guidance*. This topic can arouse tremendous controversy. There is clear teaching from Paul on submission: 'Respect those who work hard among you, who are over you in the Lord and who admonish you' (1 Thessalonians 5:12). Equally leaders must not lord it over their flock, or they will begin to lose their credentials for being leaders. They will be serving themselves rather than God. In Operation Mobilisation we meet the issue of submission fairly constantly, and those of us who are leaders do our best to appreciate an individual's sense of guidance and to pray with those under us to see what the Lord's will is. We are concerned not to be unreasonable, but to warn those under us if we see them going into situations that could get dangerous or embarking on unwise courses of action. From the viewpoint of those under authority, be careful not to follow blindly or to let the leader carry all the responsibility for guidance. That would be a cop-out, a denial of your own responsibility for understanding what the Lord is saying to you.

Guidance is one of the most difficult areas of the Christian faith, especially in big areas such as choosing a career or marriage partner. I am grateful to Dr Francis Schaeffer for pointing out that prayer is not some kind of slot machine where you put in the small change of your requests, pull the handle and click! out comes your little evangelical chocolate answered prayer, which you can show round to everyone to let them know you are spiritual. God is sometimes much more concerned with our humility or with our faith than with our prayers for this or that: you may pull the lever hundreds of times before you learn what you need to know about the way God works. We can't box God in. He will break out of all our little systems with denominational or personal labels. He is not a *tame* God.

You will already be familiar with the balance needed *between warfare and the rest of faith in the Christian life.* There is plenty of language in the Bible about fighting: 'I have fought the good fight,' says Paul to Timothy. Frankly I don't like all this military terminology, but God in his sovereignty has chosen and so I must accept it and use it, as I have in this book. Certainly we are in a war situation. At the same time our finger need not be always on the trigger. Isaiah 26:3 is a verse that has often ministered to my own heart, and I suggest that you too meditate on it frequently: 'You will keep in perfect peace him whose mind is stead-fast, because he trusts in you.' Deep trust is necessary preparation for battle.

Then, too, we need balance *between basic Christian principles and the policies of a particular church or movement*. I deal with this point at greater length in my book *A Revolution of Love and Balance*. We need to be able to discern which is which! In OM we have found that it was sensible for short-term staff during the summer to use sleeping bags, because they were moving around so much of the time. Then we had one girl who felt that sleeping bags were God's way, that they were perhaps a symbol of a nomadic existence not tied down to possessions and status, and so when she went home she asked her mother to have her bed removed from her room so that she could sleep on the floor. You can just imagine what her mother must have thought.

This may seem a nit-picking point to make, but I am amazed at how Christians can get so uptight about such trivial matters. Length of hair, style of dress, using pews or chairs in church, all can cause confusion and divison. Paul's approach is very clear as he talks of food laws: what matters is that you do as your conscience says, but always make allowances for consciences that are more uneasy than your own, for your love for your brother will include concern that he should not feel uncomfortable. Read 1 Corinthians 8:9–13.

Seek too to find a balance *between love and judgment*. 'What do you prefer?' Paul asked the Corinthians. 'Shall I come to you with a whip, or in love and with a gentle spirit?' There are times when we have to offer reproof to another believer, though always in love. Judgment is a vital part of the Christian message and from time to time particular people will feel called to speak of judgment. David Wilkerson (of *The Cross and the Switchblade* fame) is one man who feels that this should be his theme at present and some of his tapes are quite uncomfortable to listen to. Always your judgments must be motivated by love: if you cannot

110

speak hard truth in charity, then let someone else do so. You are disqualified. This is equally true whether the other person is a Christian or a nonbeliever. D L Moody's preaching was revolutionised by a little-known Englishman who pointed out that he should speak more on the subject of love. There is something in most of us that inclines towards judgment: I reckon that if we make our message and concerns 80 per cent love and 20 per cent judgment then we have the balance about right.

Some of us need to learn the balance *between work and worship*. Some feel that praising God is the be-all and end-all. Others are more anxious to get out on the streets to start the Christian revolution. Both are fine: but we find activist types (like me) joining Operation Mobilisation and then getting upset because of the hours we spend praising and worshipping. The truth of the matter is that if we are going to do an effective job then it will not be by our own might but by the Spirit of God, and hence there will be much waiting upon the Lord, and much time given over to glorifying him. Sometimes we cannot get right with God until we have got right with one another, and that too takes time. Do strive to avoid polarisation here: after polarisation comes paralysation, and the Devil is winning at every turn.

The next area has proved one of the most difficult to get right, especially for Christian leaders. It concerns the balance *between the church and the family*. On the evidence of what I observe it seems natural for Christian men to neglect their families. Here you are, preaching and guiding and counselling, and your wife and children get left out of the picture. Someone once said, 'Any fool can learn by experience.' So if you don't yet have a wife and family, try to learn from others' experience before you make the mistake for yourself, that it is very easy – and even, by a twisted way of thinking, virtuous – to neglect them. If not, you *will* learn by experience, when your wife leaves you or has a breakdown. The same man added, 'It is a wise man who learns by instruction.' The Devil in these days is putting all his might against the family, and he is going to win unless you give the

111

matter careful attention right from the start. Work at communicating, at staying in touch, especially when the pressure is on. If you are not yet married, you can still learn how to communicate. Learn how to understand different kinds of people. Learn to accept and ignore others' weaknesses: your wife to be (or your future husband) may have the same faults as your flatmate has right now. If you have leadership responsibilities it is clear from Paul's letters that one of the qualifications for your position is that your family should be obedient and respectful. Your family will not show obedience and respect towards you – let alone love – if you do not take your full share in their upbringing. Love begets love.

Try also to achieve a balance *between positive and negative*. This is a tough one, because it is so indefinable. Many people have a basically negative outlook on life, with a streak of cynicism, a tendency to look on the black side of the picture. If you feel yourself to be in that category, then let me give you three warnings: by the age of forty you are going to be a thoroughly miserable person; you are going to make a lot of other people thoroughly miserable; and I think I should be praying for whoever you end up marrying! Your children will be three times as negative and will probably end up negative about you as well. A negative spirit shows an unbelieving heart, for you are not really convinced that God can work things out. It is a contradiction to the injunction in Philippians 4:8 and 9 to think about 'whatever is true, whatever is noble, whatever is right, whatever is pure, whatever is lovely, whatever is admirable'. I realise that cynicism is a protection against the disappointments of life, but it carries a very high price tag. If you want to survive as a Christian on planet earth, where there is so much to be negative about, then you have to be able to say, 'I can do all things through Christ who strengthens me.'

There is certainly a place for negative statements, and the Bible abounds with them. There is nothing wrong with seeing the negative side provided you are prepared to work your way through to the positive side. This is an area where

I am still battling to know how to find the right balance, and there are no easy answers. There's no little tree outside my house which drops a baptism of positiveness on me as I walk underneath. It is an act of the will.

Life will be a lot easier if you can exercise a *balanced view of reckless faith and common sense*. Tozer comments, 'A bit of healthy disbelief is as needful as faith to the welfare of our souls. We would do well to cultivate a reverent scepticism: it will keep us out of a thousand bogs and quagmires. It is not fatal to doubt some things: it may well be fatal to believe everything.' Christians are called to have faith, not to be credulous. There are a lot of naïve evangelical people around who simply believe everything, especially if it sounds spiritual, or concerns a miracle, and particularly if it is in book form. A lot of people have been misled this way, and it is important to pray for discernment. Just because a man has a nice face, a good build, a pleasant manner and a reputation for being godly, that does not mean that every word he says is true. Search the word of God: use the Bible as a check for all teaching, including this book.

My last point concerns the need for balance *between anointing and training*. Some Christians place such a heavy emphasis on the need for the anointing of the Spirit that they insist that Bible schools, pastoral training and careful teaching are of the Devil. What nonsense this is! Of course we desperately need trained theologians and pastors and missionaries, especially those who are humble, broken, filled with the Spirit.

I spent two years at the Moody Bible Institute, and for me it was a most valuable time, giving me the chance to dig deep into all kinds of good spiritual books. It was at Moody that I first caught the vision of Turkey and other lands which has been such an important part of the ministry of OM. College was a time of great worth: of many temptations, but a superb growing time.

Do not think that such training will destroy your personality or force you into some kind of mould. God wants to see your personality grow – into the image of his son Jesus as you expose yourself to his Spirit and his word. Indeed, as

113

you learn more and more about his truths, and are able to take upon yourself more and more of his Spirit's blessing, you will become a *richer* personality. You will not feel the need to prove yourself so much. You will begin to become familiar with a dual vision of yourself: both as someone who falls hopelessly short of God's ideal, and someone who is a great deal nicer to know than they used to be.

In every area of our lives there is a need for some kind of balance. Do not think of balance as a dull boring concept, or in the way they consider it in some parts of the States, where all moderation and compromise is seen as of the Devil. Balance is harmony, gentleness, a stable base for building a revolution of love.

11.

FAMILY LIVING

Discipleship starts in the family: not just husband and wife, but parents and grandparents and children and grandchildren. Your family probably knows you better than anyone else in the world, certainly better than you think they do. You will not be able to keep many secrets from them, and they will see right through your pretensions. As such they are a most valuable sounding-board, apart from deserving your best efforts. A Christian home can be a glorious witness to the reality of the Lord in your midst, and also a marvellous asset in keeping your feet on the right path. If it turns sour it gives the lie to all your fine words and destroys in the bud any chance of improvement.

In this brief treatment of the subject I want to discuss some of the areas where, again, balance is needed. It is worth keeping them at the back of your mind as a warning system when in the heat of the argument you find yourself saying things you wish you could take back.

One common area where most of us could use some balance is the guilt-inducing debate about 'forsaking all' and yet maintaining an attractive home. At both ends of this spectrum I come across people who seem to me to have things wrong. Plenty of Christians give quite a high priority to decorating their home, and not infrequently I feel like asking some pointed questions about their standard of living. A number of books, such as John White's *The Golden Cow*, have appeared over the past years, and if you are worried that your standard of living is rather better than it ought to be then I would commend this one to you as well written and full of good sense. Another part of the Christian community however seems to feel that it is unspiritual to maintain an attractive home, and that it is far better to give away as much as possible for the Lord's work. Something in me has a lot of sympathy for this point of view, but it entails certain problems. A scruffy and dingy home is a poor witness to a religion that preaches joy, and it is really hard to be steadfastly cheerful, let alone happy, in ugly surroundings. Our Lord created beauty: most of what is truly ugly in the world is man-made. From this I conclude that he loves beauty, and our homes should be as beautiful as possible. How to keep this in balance when tens of millions of people across the world have no proper homes at all to speak of is an issue I am still wrestling with very deeply.

This does not mean expensively furnished. We need to see beyond the standards of our immediate neighbourhood if that neighbourhood assesses furniture by how much it cost. Most attractive homes are the result of the effort and imagination that has gone into their design rather than because of the money that has been spent. Husbands should take an interest in how their homes look and allow their wives the time and the cash to decorate as well as possible. They should also lend a generous hand. You are both liberated in Christ: try to break out of some of the social moulds, especially the one which is labelled 'little woman at home'.

In this context it is worth pointing out that it is God who is our security. Many people in the Western world considerably overspend on insurance and burglar alarms and sophisticated locks. Some insurance may be prudent: don't let it become a mania. God can look after you. We have some hundred and sixty families in OM living by faith, and their children are well provided for and they do not lack any essentials. It is so easy to fall back on secular schemes, rather than be the concerned, caring community that we should be.

A second area of family life where balance is much needed is in the relationship between being open and honest, and being kind. Of course this issue extends beyond the family context, but kindness is the absent friend all too often at many dinner tables. Honesty without love is a curse. If you feel that a member of your family needs a few home truths (telling phrase!) then be absolutely sure that they are based in and bounded by love. This equally applies to the discipline you impose on your children. Sometimes kindness overrules honesty: if you're a man then your thoughts probably stray from time to time to other women, but it might be more loving not to confess them to your wife. (Most politic as well.) You will be aware that emotional love fluctuates wildly: it can be thoroughly immature to share every passing feeling. A strong marriage is one based on dedication and commitment to one another rather than on a series of sexual or romantic highs. Constantly affirm your allegiance to your marriage partner: don't let it grow cold.

You should also balance your conviction with love. People matter more than principles for, like the Sabbath, principles exist to serve people. Thus it is sometimes more important to love than to win an argument. Your loyalty to your wife or your parents or your children should take precedence over everything, excepting only your loyalty to your Lord, should it come to that crunch (and occasionally it does). Love is not by any means soft or indulgent, and sometimes can be very hard. But be sure that if you are insisting on your convictions you are doing so aware of the best interests of your family. It is important for the husband to accept and to value his wife as she is: and it is also important for the wife to support her husband. With great gratitude I can say that my wife has always been my strongest supporter, and never once have I picked up the hint that she was not backing me all the way. Even when we disagree she can still affirm that she believes in me.

'Not enough' and 'too much' are common bugbears in marriage. If you are married or are expecting to be married some day, then the following might be a useful checklist. They are all complaints shared with me by husbands and wives over the past twenty-five years.

A. Here are the 'not enoughs':

Not enough time. Usually on the wife's lips rather than the husband's: give your marriage partner precedence over your hobbies and other friendships always, and over your Christian work unless totally unavoidable. If you have to put your Christian work first then ensure you can catch up on the talking later. Try to work as a team and to do things together.

Not enough information. Make sure you share what is on your mind. You will probably find the need to have an area of your thinking marked 'Private', but see that it is as small as possible.

Not enough money. Money, and the lack of it, will cause your bitterest arguments in all probability. Even if you keep separate bank accounts see that you discuss your expenditure together. It is most important to get this area of your life organised. Learn to trust and believe the best.

Not enough sex. Tends to be the husband's complaint rather than the wife's. So many pages have been written on this subject in the last two decades that I see little point in adding to them, except to say that the wife should absolutely never use sex as 'operation carrot'. It is utterly essential to find harmony in your sex lives. Sex can be either a great delight or a source of dreadful pain and temptation. Never be afraid to read a good book on the subject or seek counsel from others. Beware of marital pride.

Not enough affection. As men and women we often need love and affection much more than sex. Here is an area where we must not presume on one another and it would be good to think of the words of Jesus, 'Not to be ministered unto, but to minister'. Men need to remember that with women, little things, little encouragements and little expressions of affection are often more

118

meaningful than perhaps some of the big things that bring greater satisfaction to men.

Not enough water. A male problem for the most part. There is no reason why your wife should tolerate your bad breath and smelly feet. A little soap and water can go a long way. Details like this in marriage are very important.

Not enough prayer. It is often hard to pray together, especially if your individual prayer lives are not so hot. But don't give up – praying together is a wonderful centre to your marriage.

B. And now for the 'too muches':

Too many people. Quite often this is the wife's fault. She takes a bit too much pride in her hospitality and in consequence forgets the needs of her husband and children. Make sure that all those guests don't hinder something more important. For Christian leaders and pastors there is the danger of bringing too many people home.

Too much looking at other women. Men, control your eyes. Your wandering appetites can really hurt your wives. Both of you, stamp down hard on any thoughts beginning, 'If only I'd married. . .' Don't be naïve about Satan's subtle traps in this area.

Too much fat. Gluttony is such a common sin that you never hear anything about it any more. Both men and women can neglect themselves, but I see a lot of women, not quite in their first youth, who are definitely carrying too much weight. It is your husband's duty and basically his wish to love you: you will make it a lot easier for him if you keep the pounds off.

Too many children. Not necessarily in total quantity, but from time to time make sure you get away for a real break. Both you and they will benefit from it. Single people can also enjoy your family and play a real part in looking after them. If you are single, see if there is a family where you could help from time to time. Offers are rarely refused!

Too many demands. Husbands tend to become

119

fraught by meetings, and wives pay a high price for the part their husbands play if there are children to care for. Ask yourself: is my presence at that committee really needed? Is it my top priority? We easily make far too many heavy demands on each other.

Your family form your closest neighbours. Love them as yourself. If your radical discipleship does not start in the home it has not truly begun.

12.

LORD OF ALL

It is my prayer that this book will have challenged you to a deeper and richer Christian life, more outgoing and more effective. The aim of this final chapter is to encourage you in this fuller commitment and the accompanying fullness of the Holy Spirit. I am afraid it is likely that some of you who read this book will have reached this stage without saying with all their heart, 'Jesus, you are going to be Lord of everything.' I would like therefore to be specific about what 'everything' is going to mean.

Of all drugs the search for *status* is the most addictive and the least satisfying. It is also the most common. None of us is truly free of it. Yet it is directly against the whole nature of the Christian gospel, for our only claim to fame is that God has redeemed us because he loved us. 'If I must boast,' says Paul to the Corinthians, 'I will boast of the things that show my weakness.' So worry only about what Jesus is thinking about you, and ignore what others may say. If you do hear some morsel of hot juicy gossip against yourself, forget it. Just think: if they knew all the truth they'd really have something to go on! Of all the people in the world, you are the one least qualified to judge your own worth. Don't try to.

Another major area that is one of the last to be brought under the lordship of Christ is your *social life*, specifically your relationships with members of the opposite sex. (And in some cases your own sex.) Some of the most dedicated young people I have ever met have told me that their social life is badly mixed up in this respect. One minute they are leading a Christian Union meeting or talking about Jesus, and within the hour they are in bed with their girlfriend. Sometimes they are engaged in what can be classified as 'evangelical sex'. If that is a new term to you, it means not going all the way but doing everything else instead. I have had people share with me that they have gone to bed with their girlfriends or boyfriends without any clothes on, but since they didn't go all the way they didn't regard it as fornication, so their consciences have a loophole. That is a sin against the Living God – it is immorality – and you are deceiving yourself if you pretend that this is not. If you find yourself involved in heavy petting then you are going too far; you are playing with fire. If you believe you can make progress in your Christian life and still compromise in this way, even with a boy or girl that you are likely to marry, then you are in for some big surprises.

Please don't get me wrong. There is nothing against dating, or against doing sports together, going to church, taking a walk in the woods. No one is telling you that it is sinful to kiss your girlfriend goodnight – but some of you are like Jaguars with Volkswagen brakes, and you need to get them overhauled. Don't follow David's example: follow Joseph's. There was a man who made his God the absolute monarch of his life, so that even when a lovely, voluptuous Egyptian woman tried to take him to bed he could say, 'How could I do such a wicked thing and sin against God?' even though he ended up in prison.

To some extent the churches are at fault. You find churches which say with pride, 'We teach the whole counsel of God.' When did you last hear a sermon on the following passage from Proverbs 5:18–20?

> May your fountain be blessed,
>   and may you rejoice in the wife of your youth.
> A loving doe, a graceful deer –
>   may her breasts satisfy you always,

122

> may you ever be captivated by her love.
>> Why be captivated, my son, by an adulteress?
>> Why embrace the bosom of another man's wife?

You might also think about verse 23:

> He will die for lack of discipline,
>> led astray by his own great folly.

Marriage was given to us by God as one of his most lovely gifts. Sex is beautiful. Billy Graham calls it the 'creative force' within us. It is a big part of God's plan, but it has got to be according to God's pattern, within the commitment of marriage, set free because it is within limits.

Another specific area that I'd like to question is your *free time*. Is Jesus Lord of that as well? You can tell a man's maturity by what he does with his leisure, for it is then that the truth about him can be discovered. (Bookcases are very revealing. What do you read for pleasure?) There is nothing wrong with taking a couple of weeks off to go mountaineering, or sailing, or to lie on a beach. But you can't take a couple of weeks off from being a Christian, because the Devil doesn't take holidays. If you're not careful your leisure time can lay you open to all kinds of temptations.

One of the commonest is simply wasting time. Without discipline and crucifixion of the self-life you are likely to waste hundreds of God's precious hours. You will know from some of the things I've said in earlier chapters that I am all for relaxing: every Christian should have a hobby and a sport. 'God has given us all things richly to enjoy.' But relaxing, to my mind, does not mean hanging about chatting or flipping through some silly magazines or watching an idle television show. You are merely passing time and only occupying the surface of your mind. Find things you really enjoy and put all you've got into them. I don't necessarily mean violent activity: it might mean dreaming on a tree stump somewhere in a wood. Learn how to savour your pleasures. Real pleasure, as C S Lewis points out in

The Screwtape Letters, is a splendid defence against the attacks of Satan.

Television is a particular problem. I don't think I'm neurotic about television, though I have been heard to say that the best place to hang your prayer map of the world is in front of the screen. A television is a useful thing to have: there is news to pray about, there are Christian programmes, there are good plays and documentaries and sports. But so easily the television can end up controlling you. Recently I visited a dear friend whom I hadn't seen in some years and they couldn't even turn off the football game when I walked into their living room. There is nothing at all wrong with football games, but as so often in the Christian life the good can become the enemy of the best. Be self-critical about your use of the box.

Make Jesus Christ Lord of your *future*. What are you going to do with your life? God does not tell everyone to leave their nets, and in fact most 'full-time' Christian workers are the more effective for having spent a few years in an office or school or on a shop floor. But be quite clear that Jesus owns those nets.

I had some very nice 'nets'. At the age of sixteen I owned three small businesses. I was a little visionary capitalist and I had 200 people working for me part time: my vision involved doing the least work possible, instead letting other people do it for me. I owned a philatelic agency, a firefighting equipment business and one other small setup. It was great to have pockets full of money, and to go to New York night clubs and blow it all in one evening.

Then one day I was prayed into a Billy Graham meeting, and sat there, in Madison Square Garden, a little middle-class bourgeois American pagan, and met the man from Galilee.

From that moment I never knew anything except total surrender to Jesus (an ongoing process!) There was no other option. I cannot understand how people can make a big thing of committing their lives to Christ and just go on as they did before, with only a few minor changes. Faith in Jesus Christ is a radical thing. When you meet the Saviour he gives you a complete overhaul. You never know how much time you have left to serve him, so your talents, your strength, your energy, your mind, your hour by hour existence all count for eternity.

In view of this, what are you going to do? Will you find a nice job, a nice house and a nice car, with a nice mortgage? Keep up with the other families in the road, and of course go to church because it is respectable and in America at least you can make good business contacts? (Especially if you're an undertaker.) Jesus is not respectable: but he does care if you're at odds with anyone in your fellowship when you break bread together. He is the one 'from whom no secrets are hid'. It is far more important to live in love and unity with one another than to maintain appearances. Do not clothe yourself in cold respectability, but rather take part in operation defrost as the warm love of our Saviour melts your hearts. And as the ice melts, you may perhaps hear his voice saying 'Follow me, I want to make you a fisher of men.' Keep listening! He may be calling some of you to good secular employment, not least to earn the money to give to support those in full-time work; but also simply to be a Christian presence in the market places of the world. The important thing is to be ready to hear and to obey.

Give over into Jesus's care as well all your *material possessions*. I have made a few comments on this in the previous chapter, so for the moment I will only say that probably just about everyone who reads this book should be classified as a rich young ruler by comparison with the majority of people in the world. The comparison is valid: Solzhenitsyn said, 'To talk about internal affairs in the present world is just ridiculous.' Do not compare yourself with those in America or Germany or anywhere else that has a higher standard of living; they are the few. (Incidentally, do not judge them for their higher standards: many of them have a greater love for Jesus than you do.) Set yourself free from the shackles of material things: make Christ Lord over your cheque book and credit card and that inheritance you have just received. It is a beautiful experience to be set free from clinging to possessions. 'My God will meet all your needs according to his glorious riches in Christ Jesus' (Philippians 4:19).

Shortly after I was converted my parents and my sister also found the Lord. God was just starting to work through me, and my father told me that I needed a new car for my ministry. (At that point I was driving a fifteen-year-old truck. We repaired it, and it did another 50,000 miles.) 'Dad,' I told him, 'I can't take a new car when there are so many other needs. We need Bibles! Tracts! There are Mexicans who don't have a place to live. They don't have any food on their tables.' So my father, then in his fifties, (a hard-working electrician) began to get a vision for giving his money for Christian literature and other works of God overseas, a vision that so few seem to have in our day. He had only just become a true believer but God was working in his life. He and my mother even moved into a smaller home in order to give more money to get the gospel out.

When a revival moved through Canada, farmers put large chunks of land aside and dedicated it to world evangelism. There is one farmer out in Colorado who has dedicated a cow and everything it produces to the work of spreading the gospel.

In the same way, see that your possessions are under the Lord's control. 'This is how we know what love is: Jesus Christ laid down his life for us. And we ought to lay down our lives for our brothers. If anyone has material possessions and sees his brother in need but has no pity on him, how can the love of God be in him?' (1 John 3:16,17). Possessions include skills. There is tremendous need in missionary work for people who can handle computers, for bookkeepers, for mechanics, for engineers, for radio technicians. God also needs the one-talent men – and if you only have one talent, then praise him, you have less to take care of! You may find it difficult to communicate. You may even be handicapped. I think of a man in Chicago who had no arms or legs, and was also blind: yet he learned to read the braille Bible with his tongue, had a radiant testimony for God and taught the word of God wonderfully. Of Joni,

126

an ordinary schoolgirl who would never have been known in the world apart from her own friends in Maryland, but because of a terrible accident she has already been used to touch millions for Christ.

No matter how little you have, Jesus can use it. D L Moody was described by a secular encyclopedia as a man who 'depopulated hell by two million souls'. One day the Lord touched Moody in New England, a man who couldn't even speak proper English, and asked 'What is that in your hand?' 'Just shoes, Lord,' said Moody. He was a shoe salesman. God asked the same question of William Carey, the pioneer Baptist missionary to India. 'Just shoes, Lord,' answered Carey. He was a cobbler. 'Give them to me,' commanded the Lord, and Carey did so. Whether you make shoes or microchips, God can use you. Thank him if you can for your body, for health, for energy, for every asset you can think of, and turn them over to his care.

As a true believer you are God's child. Jesus is within you. To you, to everyone, he is saying, 'I want to be your Lord, I want to be the king of your life. I want to control your time, your talents, your money, your holidays, your work, your marriage. Come to me, to the foot of the cross, and make me Lord of your life.'

RECOMMENDED READING

The Spirit-Controlled Temperament, Tim LaHaye, Kingsway
Eros Defiled, John White, Inter-Varsity Press
The Calvary Road, Roy Hession, Christian Literature Crusade
Healing for Damaged Emotions, David Seamands, Scripture
    Press
Evidence that Demands a Verdict Volume 1, Josh MacDowell,
    Scripture Press
Evidence that Demands a Verdict Volume 2, Josh MacDowell,
    Scripture Press
Knowing God, J I Packer, Hodder and Stoughton
Parents in Pain, John White, Inter-Varsity Press
From Now On..., Ralph Shallis, OM Publishing
Spiritual Depression, Martyn Lloyd-Jones, Marshall Pickering